D0849083

NANCY PELOSI

Recent Titles in Greenwood Biographies

Steven Spielberg: A Biography
Kathi Jackson

Madonna: A Biography
Mary Cross

Jackie Robinson: A Biography
Mary Kay Linge

Bob Marley: A Biography
David V. Moskowitz

Sitting Bull: A Biography
Edward J. Rielly

Eleanor Roosevelt: A Biography
Cynthia M. Harris

Jesse Owens: A Biography
Jacqueline Edmondson

The Notorious B.I.G.: A Biography
Holly Lang

Hillary Clinton: A Biography
Dena B. Levy and Nicole R. Krassas

Johnny Depp: A Biography
Michael Blitz

Judy Blume: A Biography
Kathleen Tracy

Nelson Mandela: A Biography
Peter Limb

Lebron James: A Biography
Lew Freedman

NANCY PELOSI

A Biography

Elaine S. Povich

GREENWOOD BIOGRAPHIES

GREENWOOD PRESS
WESTPORT, CONNECTICUT • LONDON

Library of Congress Cataloging-in-Publication Data

Povich, Elaine S.
    Nancy Pelosi : a biography / by Elaine S. Povich.
       p. cm. — (Greenwood biographies, ISSN 1540–4900)
    Includes bibliographical references and index.
    ISBN 978–0–313–34570–8 (alk. paper)
    1. Pelosi, Nancy, 1940– 2. Women legislators—United States—Biography.
3. Legislators—United States—Biography. 4. United States. Congress.
House—Biography. 5. United States. Congress. House—Speakers—Biography.
6. Women in politics—United States—Biography. 7. United States—Politics and
government—1989– 8. California—Politics and government—1951– I. Title.
    E840.8.P37P68 2008
    328.73092—dc22
    [B]   2008012987

British Library Cataloging in Publication Data is available.

Library of Congress Catalog Card Number: 2008012987
ISBN: 978–0–313–34570–8
ISSN: 1540–4900

First published in 2008

Greenwood Press, 88 Post Road West, Westport, CT 06881
An imprint of Greenwood Publishing Group, Inc.
www.greenwood.com

Printed in the United States of America

The paper used in this book complies with the
Permanent Paper Standard issued by the National
Information Standards Organization (Z39.48–1984).

10 9 8 7 6 5 4 3 2 1

To the memory of Dad, and to Ron, Mark, and Kenny—men who knew, and know, that women can do anything. And to Mom, who knows we all need a little help.

CONTENTS

CONTENTS

Photo essay follows page 80

SERIES FOREWORD

In response to high school and public library needs, Greenwood developed this distinguished series of full-length biographies specifically for student use. Prepared by field experts and professionals, these engaging biographies are tailored for high school students who need challenging yet accessible biographies. Ideal for secondary school assignments, the length, format and subject areas are designed to meet educators' requirements and students' interests.

Greenwood offers an extensive selection of biographies spanning all curriculum-related subject areas including social studies, the sciences, literature and the arts, history and politics, as well as popular culture, covering public figures and famous personalities from all time periods and backgrounds, both historic and contemporary, who have made an impact on American and/or world culture. Greenwood biographies were chosen based on comprehensive feedback from librarians and educators. Consideration was given to both curriculum relevance and inherent interest. The result is an intriguing mix of the well known and the unexpected, the saints and sinners from long-ago history and contemporary pop culture. Readers will find a wide array of subject choices from fascinating crime figures like Al Capone to inspiring pioneers like Margaret Mead, from the greatest minds of our time like Stephen Hawking to the most amazing success stories of our day like J. K. Rowling.

While the emphasis is on fact, not glorification, the books are meant to be fun to read. Each volume provides in-depth information about the subject's life from birth through childhood, the teen years, and adulthood.

A thorough account relates family background and education, traces personal and professional influences, and explores struggles, accomplishments, and contributions. A timeline highlights the most significant life events against a historical perspective. Bibliographies supplement the reference value of each volume.

ACKNOWLEDGMENTS

No book can be written alone, even if only one name is listed as "author." I was lucky to have the assistance of an incredible number of dedicated friends and associates who provided much needed support and counsel in the writing of this book. I would like to thank the incomparable Jim Toedtman, my editor in a couple of incarnations, who first assigned me the story on House Speaker Nancy Pelosi that became the catalyst for this book and who provided much needed guidance and encouragement.

John Burton, politician extraordinaire, with a gruff exterior and an indefatigable spirit, gave me an unparalleled look into Pelosi's political life and those of his brother, Phil, and his sister-in-law, Sala, her predecessors in Congress and her mentors. I would like to thank Marty and Liz Weld Nolan and the members of the Sacramento Seminar for welcoming me to their convivial luncheon and for giving me a lively primer on the complexities of California politics. Ed Moose, of Moose's Restaurant in San Francisco, spun out political tales over great food and drink.

Gil Sandler, an unrivaled Baltimore historian, gave me a wonderful perspective on the colorful history of Baltimore. Tommy D'Alesandro III revealed unique insights into his sister Nancy and the whole D'Alesandro family. Angie and John Guerriero opened their home in Baltimore's "Little Italy" to me and provided historical context of the neighborhood where Pelosi grew up. Sally Laughland opened her Institute of Notre Dame yearbooks for me and took me on a virtual tour of the school in the 1950s.

Johnny Miller and the *San Francisco Chronicle* library provided comprehensive background material and allowed me to relive the grand old days of dusty and clunky microfiche machines. The Enoch Pratt library in Baltimore, along with Karen Hosler and the *Baltimore Sun* Library, dug deep into their archives for me. U.S. Senate Librarian Greg Harness and his staff were quick to find any information I needed, even if it was on the "other body" of Congress, the House.

Michael Yaki, Pelosi's first chief of staff, made me feel like I was present at the creation of a rising star in Congress with his lively descriptions.

The book benefited from the suggestions of Jack Torry, journalist, author, and narrative style maven. Marie Cocco, columnist, dear friend, and confidant, was there at the beginning of this book and was always willing to talk me through the tough times. Steve Daley, a stylish writer, provided contacts, inspiration, and some deft suggestions. Thanks to Sharon Kaufman, the best best-friend ever, for her knowledge of the publishing industry and for being my No. 1 fan. Thanks to Jon Kimball and the St. Francis Hotel in San Francisco, which sure beats a garret as a place to write.

The articles of Marc Sandalow and Ed Epstein, both formerly of the *San Francisco Chronicle*, were the most comprehensive on Pelosi of any I found and added immeasurably to my knowledge. My friends in the House Press Gallery came up with insights and analyses that were helpful.

Thanks to my editors at *National Journal's Congress Daily*, especially Kathy Gambrell, Keith White, and Lou Peck, for giving me the time to write when I needed it most.

I am indebted to Brendan Daly, communications director for Nancy Pelosi, who was never too busy to check a fact, handle a request, or steer me in the right direction.

A very special thanks to Sandy Towers of Greenwood Publishing Group for initiating this project and for being willing to work so seamlessly with me throughout.

Personal thanks to my wonderful husband, Ron Dziengiel, and my terrific sons, Mark and Kenny Dziengiel, for putting up with take-out food, seeing lots of movies, and going on many outings to give me time to write and for tolerating this uninvited guest in our home who competed mercilessly for my attention at times when my family needed me the most.

And, finally, thanks to the extraordinary Nancy D'Alesandro Pelosi who, like Ginger Rogers dancing with Fred Astaire, does everything her male counterparts do—backwards and in high heels.[1]

NOTE

1. Bob Thaves, 1982 © NEA Inc. "Frank and Ernest" Cartoon, May 3, 1982.

INTRODUCTION

On January 4, 2007, the Speaker of the United States House of Representatives ascended to the podium before a packed chamber and took the oath of office. The ritual had been repeated by 59 other Speakers in the history of the United States of America, but this time was different: Nancy D'Alesandro Pelosi became the first woman Speaker of the House.

Her face radiated pure joy as she took the gavel handed to her by House Minority Leader John Boehner of Ohio and raised it over her head in triumph. That gavel represented more than just leadership. With her oath of office, Pelosi broke what she called the "marble ceiling" that had kept women out of the top post in the U.S. House since 1789. It was one of the last bastions of all-male rule and one that had been particularly difficult to crack. Women had held high office before—governors, senators, presidential Cabinet officials—but never the highest office in Congress.

With Pelosi's ascension to Speaker in 2007, the only higher offices never to have been held by a woman were president and vice president. With her Speakership, another barrier on the road to political equality was broken.

There were cheers and emotional tears in the House that day. Even her Republican rivals, such as Rep. Boehner, could not help but mark the history-making occasion. Women of both parties were particularly joyful, just to see one of their own presiding.

As the applause and cheers deepened and cascaded across the cavernous, ornate chamber, Pelosi did one other thing that had never before been done. She called her grandchildren up to surround her at the podium and then extended a similar invitation to all of the children in the House who had come to witness their parents' and grandparents' swearing-in as members of Congress.

Little feet mounted the steep podium. Pelosi's infant grandson, Paul Michael Vos, slept in the arms of his eight-year-old cousin, Madeleine Prowda, oblivious to the historic moment. But the awe in the other children's eyes was obvious. Maybe, they must have thought, maybe I could do this one day, too. And the tableau that day served visual notice that this was to be a Speakership like no other.

Pelosi's theme that day was children.

Pelosi had not started out to be a trailblazer. Her path to the post that is second in the line of succession to the presidency had not been single-minded—she was a wife, a mother of five, and a grandmother of seven. She served in the Democratic Party's "trenches" while her children were growing up, doing the spade work of political party planning–running get-out-the-vote drives, stuffing envelopes, organizing rallies. She never really planned to run for public office, but the death of a close friend who was a member of Congress thrust her into a race for the House, where her "inexperience" and youthful looks were held against her.

Yet politics was in her blood. Her father, Thomas D'Alesandro, Jr., was a New Deal Democrat when she was born on March 26, 1940. When she was seven, he won the first of three terms as Baltimore's mayor. Her brother, Thomas D'Alesandro III, followed him and also became mayor.

Nancy Pelosi had an innate talent for public service. When she was 13, she was asked to work the desk at the "Mayor's Open House" day, when, once a week, Mayor D'Alesandro opened his home to constituents who came into their dining room with problems, questions, or requests. Nancy's five older brothers had the job of running the desk until she was old enough to do it. But once that happened, she proved to be so good at it that her brothers eventually relinquished the task to her.

She was not a particularly spectacular speaker; she didn't wow crowds with her ease and banter. What she did have was an uncanny ability to create political coalitions and an indefatigable ability to raise money and campaign. Once established as the congresswoman from San Francisco, she turned her efforts to helping others in the House. Over her career, she did favors and raised money for so many Democrats that they all knew her—and most liked her. Even those who didn't admired her tenacity and energy.

Pelosi's path to leadership was not smooth. She had to fight off challenges from other House members who wanted the leadership posts as much as, if not more than, she did. But she continued working tirelessly, racking up chits and favors as she went along, at times sleeping only five or six hours a night.

She continued to balance family and work, even as her children matured and became parents of their own, making her a proud grandmother as well as Speaker of the House.

She never gave up. She used her political instincts and talents to fight for what she believed in, no matter the odds. When she became leader of the Democrats in the House, down one rung from the top, she wanted more. "I want to be Speaker," she declared. She weathered adversity and challenge, with a fighting spirit, boundless energy—and a weakness for chocolate.

Nancy D'Alesandro Pelosi, Speaker of the United States House of Representatives: She ascended to the top position in the United States Congress, and she continues to inspire women of all ages who want to make a political difference.

TIMELINE: EVENTS IN
THE LIFE OF NANCY PELOSI

March 26, 1940	Born Nancy Patricia D'Alesandro in the Little Italy section of Baltimore, the only daughter and youngest of six children of Thomas and Annunciata D'Alesandro.
May 1947	Thomas D'Alesandro, Jr., begins the first of three four-year terms as mayor of Baltimore.
1957	Meets U.S. Senator John F. Kennedy while attending a formal dinner with her father.
1962	Graduates from Trinity College, now Trinity University, in Washington, D.C.
September 7, 1963	Marries Paul Pelosi of San Francisco, who has graduated from Georgetown University. The couple move to New York.
1964–1970	The Pelosis have five children, Nancy Corinne, Christine, Jacqueline, Paul, and Alexandra, in a six-year span, moving to San Francisco in 1969. Nancy volunteers for Democratic candidates and causes.
1967–1971	Pelosi's brother, Thomas D'Alesandro, III, wins election as mayor of Baltimore, serving one term.
1970s	As her children grow older, Pelosi continues her Democratic Party work and becomes a proficient fundraiser.

1976   Manages California Gov. Jerry Brown's Democratic presidential primary campaign in Maryland. Brown carries the state but loses the party's nomination to Jimmy Carter.

1977–1981   Serves as northern chairwoman for the California Democratic Party.

1981   Is elected for a two-year term as state Democratic Party chairwoman.

1984   Chairs the host committee for the Democratic Party's national presidential convention in San Francisco.

1985   Serves as finance chairwoman for the national Democratic Senatorial Campaign Committee.

1987   Runs for the congressional seat representing San Francisco after the death of the incumbent, Sala Burton, who, with her late husband, longtime Representative Phil Burton, had been among Pelosi's political mentors.

April 7, 1987   Wins a closely contested Democratic primary and becomes the party's nominee in the special election to complete Sala Burton's two-year term in the House.

June 2, 1987   Pelosi, who has spent more than $1 million on her campaign, wins election to the House with 62 percent of the vote in the overwhelmingly Democratic district. A week later, she is sworn into office.

1990s   Takes up the banner of human rights in China, sponsoring measures to allow Chinese students to remain in the United States after the Tiananmen Square massacre, and tries, without success, to end China's favored trade status. As a member of the Appropriations Committee, helps lead an effort to increase federal funding for programs to research AIDS and provide services for those suffering from the disease.

1998   As a member of the House Intelligence Committee, travels to Guatemala to investigate the assassination of an activist Roman Catholic bishop, Juan Gerardi Conedera.

1999 Welcomes the first of seven grandchildren (as of 2008). Announces a campaign to run for majority whip.

2001 Becomes the top-ranking Democrat on the Intelligence Committee.

October 10, 2001 Is elected minority whip, the highest congressional party position reached by a woman to that date, defeating rival Rep. Steny Hoyer of Maryland, 118–95. She takes her post on Jan. 15, 2002.

October 10, 2002 Splits with the party's House leader, Rep. Dick Gephardt, and leads 126 Democratic votes against the resolution authorizing President Bush to use military force against Iraq. The measure nevertheless passes, 296–133.

November 14, 2002 House Democrats elect Pelosi, 177–29, as their minority leader, making her the highest ranking woman in the history of the House

November 2, 2004 President Bush wins re-election, and Pelosi is stunned when her Democrats lose seats in the House, giving the Republicans a 15-seat margin of control.

2005 Bush, after his successful re-election, introduces a plan to change Social Security and create private investment accounts. Pelosi and the Democratic leadership fight the plan, holding their caucus together, and make Bush's plan so unpopular it never even reaches the House floor.

November 2005 Rep. John Murtha, D-Pa., a conservative former Marine, announces his opposition to the war, urging Bush to begin to withdraw American troops. Pelosi endorses his proposal and uses it as a theme going into the 2006 midterm congressional elections.

2006 Pelosi campaigns across the country for Democratic candidates, raising millions of dollars in an effort to win a Democratic majority in the House.

November 7, 2006 Democrats win 30 Republican House seats to take control of the body for the first time since 1994, positioning Pelosi to become the first woman Speaker of the House.

November 16, 2006   The Democratic caucus in the House unanimously selects Pelosi as its choice for Speaker in the 110th Congress.

January 4, 2007   Pelosi elected Speaker of the U.S. House of Representatives.

Sources: San Francisco Chronicle, AARP Bulletin.

Chapter 1

BALTIMORE BEGINNINGS

At high noon on May 20, 1947, in Baltimore's War Memorial Plaza, seven-year-old Nancy D'Alesandro solemnly lifted up a family Bible in which she had written, "Dear Daddy, I hope this holy book will guide you to be a good man." Her father, Thomas "Tommy the Elder" D'Alesandro, Jr., put his left hand on the Bible, raised his right hand, and was sworn in as the mayor of Baltimore, with Nancy at his side.

Holding the Bible chest high so that her father could reach it without stooping, and focusing her eyes on him, "Little Nancy" never imagined on that day that she would be following in her father's footsteps into elected office. Yet the look in her eyes showed that she was infused with political blood.

Nancy mostly sought to emulate her mother, Annunciata, and work in the background of politics. Her life started out that way. But fate and hard work intervened, and the little girl who had started out wanting to be like her mother instead became more and more like her father. She used the political skills honed by both of her parents and went further than they could have dreamed.

The City of Baltimore is nicknamed "Charm City." But it is also a place of steel and grit. "Little Nancy" D'Alesandro, the charming girl who would grow up to be the steely Nancy Pelosi, the first woman Speaker of the U.S. House of Representatives, embodied both sides of her home-town. The combination was unstoppable.

Nancy Patricia D'Alesandro was born March 26, 1940, as World War II raged in Europe but nearly two years before the Japanese attack on Pearl Harbor, Hawaii, would bring the United States fully into the war. Woody

Woodpecker and Elmer Fudd were the popular cartoons of the day, and the Disney movie *Pinocchio* played at single-screen theaters. And the McDonald brothers opened their first restaurant that year.

At home, her father, Thomas J. D'Alesandro, Jr., was a member of the U.S. Congress at the time of her birth.

A veteran "New Dealer," in the mold of President Franklin D. Roosevelt, who coined the phrase, D'Alesandro was a foot soldier in Roosevelt's effort to revive the American economy and enhance government's efforts to provide work, economic assistance, and retirement income (Social Security) for the people.[1] He believed, as many big-city Democrats did at that time, that government existed to help people.

He infused all of his children with those beliefs. "Little Nancy," named for her mother, Annunciata, who was also called "Nancy," was the youngest of six children and the only girl. Brothers Thomas J. D'Alesandro III ("Young Tommy," who would grow up to be the mayor of Baltimore as well), Franklin Delano Roosevelt D'Alesandro (called "Roosey"), Hector D'Alesandro, Nicholas D'Alesandro, and Joseph D'Alesandro preceded her in the family.

While her father ran for public office and ran the City of Baltimore, her mother stayed home, raised the children, and volunteered in Democratic politics. When Nancy was growing up as the daughter of the mayor, their home on Albemarle Street, in the "Little Italy" section of Baltimore, was the unofficial constituent service office.

John Pente remembers the days when Mayor "Tommy the Elder" D'Alesandro got him his first job. At age 97, he still recalled the day in 1930 that he graduated from Calvert Hall High School in Baltimore with a diploma but no job prospects. "He [D'Alesandro] got me a job as a timekeeper [on city construction jobs]," Pente said.

And Pente remembered the D'Alesandro home, at the corner of Albemarle and Fawn Streets (now renamed Via Nancy D'Alesandro Pelosi), which was always bustling with people. "His home was always occupied," Pente recalled. "They would invite everybody, and they would always have people in."[2]

"Tommy the Elder" spent 22 years in public service, from state delegate to city councilman, to U.S. congressman to mayor; these posts were followed by federal appointments made by President John F. Kennedy. All the while, he was working the political system for the people who needed help, and Nancy watched.

"It was always about the progressive economic agenda for a fair economy, where many Americans, all Americans, could participate in the economic success of our country," Pelosi said on the day the street was named for her, just before her installation as Speaker in 2007. "What I got from them was about economic fairness."[3]

D'Alesandro ran the city like a lot of big-city mayors of the day—he didn't take any grief from anyone. During a city garbage strike in 1956, the Teamsters tried to strong-arm the mayor, but he did not give in. D'Alesandro had declared that striking garbage collectors, who were all Teamsters, would be fired if they did not return to work. That statement prompted a visit by a Teamsters official sent by Jimmy Hoffa himself, the president of the union and a man thought to have ties to organized crime. The official said Hoffa was "unhappy" with the mayor, an implication that bad things could happen if the mayor resisted. D'Alesandro was not intimidated, telling the official to go back to Mr. Hoffa and report that the mayor was "unhappy" with the garbage piling up in his streets. By Monday, the strike was mostly over.[4]

In 1954, a small scandal emerged involving D'Alesandro. A parking garage contractor named Dominic Piracci—who had ties to D'Alesandro even before his daughter married Tommy D'Alesandro III—was convicted of fraud and conspiracy to obstruct justice. While D'Alesandro was not implicated directly in the case, it helped to derail his career in elective office. He was defeated for renomination as mayor in 1958 and also mounted an unsuccessful campaign for the U.S. Senate that year. But D'Alesandro stayed involved politics for many years afterward.[5]

"Tommy the Elder" never moved out of Little Italy. Even when he was mayor, the limo came to his house to carry him to City Hall. Years later, he would be sitting on his steps in shorts, looking like a retired truck driver.

He was always looking to help people.

"If he [D'Alesandro] could do it, he would help," recalled Angie Guerriero, who was born in Little Italy and went to school with Pelosi's brothers and knew her as a "little kid."[6]

All the little kids in Little Italy, including Nancy, went to St. Leo's Catholic School, run by the church on the corner. They were in and out of each other's homes all the time, giving the Little Italy neighborhood, while smack in the middle of downtown Baltimore, the look and feel of a little village. People still talk about Tommy the Elder's marriage to Annunciata at St. Leo's on Sept. 30, 1928. It was to be known from then on in Little Italy as "Tommy's Wedding Day," right up there with the twin festivals of Little Italy: St. Gabriel's Festival, in August, and St. Anthony's Festival, in June.[7]

Those festivals brought out the best of the Italian American Catholic community in Little Italy. While the number of participants dwindled over the years as Little Italy shrank in population and became something of a tourist attraction, the enthusiasm for the festivals never faded. St. Gabriel's, in particular, was an enthusiastic parade of flags, religious leaders, and supporters of St. Leo's Church.

Back in 1928, the D'Alesandro wedding lasted all day and into the night. Hundreds of people streamed in and out of the Lombardi and D'Alesandro homes and the Lehmann's Hall, social building, where the reception was held. "I've been working for two years to put this wedding over, and it's gone over with a bang. They won't forget this party," Tommy was quoted at the time.[8]

Little Italy has never forgotten Tommy, nor has his daughter forgotten Little Italy or her father.

"She got her understanding of precinct politics from her father's world, watching big city political organizations at work," said Gilbert Sandler, a Baltimore historian and writer.[9]

"Our whole lives were politics," Pelosi told an interviewer during her first race for Congress, a special election she squeaked through in 1987. "If you entered the house, it was always campaign time, and if you went into the living room, it was always constituent time."[10]

When you came into the house, the front room was taken up by a constituent service office, and the desk was run by the D'Alesandro children. "Young Tommy" recalled that each of the brothers took a turn at the desk until it was Little Nancy's turn.

"When Nancy was 12 or 13 she took over," D'Alesandro said "We built up our organization with favors. It was a chore that we all did, and it wasn't really a chore. We took it for granted and we did it.

"We had our instructions—get as much detail as we could," D'Alesandro recalled. "My mother was overseer and saw to it that we handled the office."[11]

Nancy got really good at the job. So good, in fact, that her brothers stopped working there and handed the task off to Nancy altogether. She collected requests and passed them on to her mother, and they were fulfilled. With those gestures, the D'Alesandro family bought loyalty, something that Nancy would grow up to use to her own advantage. She always remembered the constituent service desk and how it was used to help people.

As she grew, her independent streak became obvious, even in relation to church.

"I didn't think I wanted to be a nun," she said. "But I thought I might want to be a priest. There seemed to be a little more power there, a little more discretion over what was going on in the parish."[12]

When she was a teenager, she recruited friends to go to a book signing by a handsome young senator who came to Baltimore. The senator was John F. Kennedy, the future president. And the book was *Profiles in Courage*, for which he would win a Pulitzer Prize.

Also as a teenager, Nancy was seated at a formal dinner at the head table next to the up-and-coming Senator Kennedy. As she tells the story, some of her teenage friends came up and asked her to sit with them at their table instead. But she declined, figuring that sitting next to the future president was a once-in-a-lifetime event. "I was really torn, but I thought perhaps I could do that [sit with friends] another day," she recalled. Her friends would have to wait.[13]

After her primary school years, Nancy went to the Institute of Notre Dame for high school. An all-girls Catholic school, it was then run by the School Sisters of Notre Dame, an order of nuns, and was known for a rather strict environment. Nancy was reserved, but not shy. She got good grades and made the National Honor Society. She was vice president of the student government in her senior year (a precursor of things to some) and was a member of the "Sodality" service club. In addition, she participated on the debate club, the French club, the Latin club, and the glee club (even though years later she would profess that she couldn't really sing very well). She was in a "fashion show" in which the girls modeled various forms of nun's habits—something she never actually wanted to wear. There were lots of pictures of her in the yearbook, including one in which she modeled the class ring.

Her prominent appearances may have been due to her status as the mayor's daughter. The yearbook also includes a picture of Mayor D'Alesandro handing out awards for extemporaneous speaking to two girls. Nancy was not one of them.

"The influence of the school on us speaks so well of who we are," said Sally Gatchell Laughland, a classmate who knew Nancy growing up.[14]

Described in her senior picture section as "pleasant and sincere" and "tres feminine" in French, her quotation was "I haven't opened a book yet," which probably was a joke, since she was good at academics.

She was pictured in a black sweater with a white Peter Pan collar, as were all of the other girls in the class.

Classmates remembered her as someone who really didn't want to stand out, possibly because she already was a semicelebrity as the daughter of the mayor. She tried to blend in with the girls. But it wasn't easy.

Every day, her father's limousine would pull up to the house in Little Italy to take the mayor to work and Nancy to school, since the two buildings were close to each other in downtown Baltimore. While the mayor apparently liked having his daughter ride with him on school days, Nancy was not at all happy about the special treatment.

Nancy insisted that the big black limo drop her off a block away from the school so that she could walk the last block and save the embarrassment of getting out of the limo as her classmates watched.

"She never did like that limo," recalled her brother Tommy.[15]

The Institute of Notre Dame in Baltimore also was the alma mater of another prominent politician from Maryland, U.S. Sen. Barbara Mikulski, although they were there at different times.

The school is proud to be the incubator of women politicians, and Sister Mary Fitzgerald, former president of the Institute of Notre Dame, said students there have been inspired by the political legacy of Pelosi and Mikulski.

"It's truly an honor to have two women in such outstanding positions in the U.S. Congress," she said. "It's not every day that a school has that."[16]

Nancy's graduation from the Institute of Notre Dame was a proud day for her and her family. She wore a white gown with a blue sash and carried a bouquet of a dozen long-stemmed red roses.

She had plans for after graduation that set her apart from the family. Unlike all of her brothers, who had chosen to go to college in Baltimore, she ventured what was then an unheard-of distance: the 40 miles to Washington, D.C., to attend Trinity College.

"It was a big step for somebody in my family," recalled her brother Tommy. "Trinity? We all went to Loyola or Calvert Hall."[17]

Nancy's father was dead set against her going to Trinity. But Annunciata had other ideas for her only daughter. Annunciata had some experience with defying family, as well. When Annunciata was a young woman in the 1920s, she was an auctioneer in Baltimore, at first sneaking out of the house to do her job. And later, once her family found out about it, she went against their wishes. Annunciata was the first woman auctioneer in Baltimore City, and she got so good at it that the company she worked for wanted to send her to New York to work there.

However, the family was having none of it, and Annunciata was prevented from taking the job in New York. Perhaps that experience was in the back of her mind when she decided to let Nancy pursue her dream of attending Trinity.

"Whatever Nancy wanted, my mother made sure that she got," recalled her brother.[18]

So it was off to Washington for Nancy, to go to school at Trinity, another incubator for successful women.

NOTES

1. University of Baltimore, Langsdale Library Special Collection.

2. John Pente, interview with author, Baltimore, June 17, 2007.

3. Lynne Duke, "Nancy Pelosi Learned Her Politics at the Elbow of Her Father the Mayor," *Washington Post,* November 10, 2006, p. C 1.

4. Ibid.

5. "The Little World of Tommy," *Time* Magazine, April 26, 1954.

6. Angie Guerriero, interview with author, June 17, 2007, Baltimore, MD.

7. Gilbert Sandler, *The Neighborhood, The Story of Baltimore's Little Italy* (Baltimore, Md.: Bodine & Associates, 1974), p. 33.

8. Ibid., pp. 34–35.

9. Gilbert Sandler, interview with author, July 19, 2007.

10. Mark Z. Barabak, "Triumph of the 'Airhead,'" *Los Angeles Times Magazine,* January 26, 2003, p. 12.

11. Thomas D'Alesandro III, interview with author, Baltimore, August 14, 2007.

12. Joe Feurerherd, "Roots in faith, family and party guide Pelosi's move to power," interview with Pelosi, *National Catholic Reporter,* January 24, 2003.

13. NBC "Today" program, Jan. 4, 2005, interview.

14. Sally Laughland, interview with author, Timonium, Md., Dec. 10, 2007.

15. Thomas D'Alesandro III, interview with author, Baltimore, August 14, 2007.

16. Kelly Brewington, "Pride of Baltimore," *Baltimore Sun,* Nov. 9, 2006, p. 1.

17. Thomas D'Alesandro III, interview with author, Baltimore, August 14, 2007.

18. Ibid.

Chapter 2

COLLEGE AND MARRIAGE

Trinity College was a new experience for Nancy. Now away from the warm circle of her parents, family, and "The Neighborhood," Nancy was on her own to experience all Trinity College had to offer. By all accounts, she took full advantage of it.

It was "all of 38 miles, but a long way for my family," Pelosi said. "My father was very old school, and there was this thinking that the children should stay home."[1]

That attitude would surface again when Nancy married and eventually moved to California. "We might as well have gone to Australia," she said.[2]

An institution for the higher education of Catholic women, Trinity was founded in 1897 by the Sisters of Notre Dame de Namur, who had settled in Washington. Its founding documents called for the institution to be "equal in its efficiency" to other women's colleges in the United States. The administrators of Catholic University, an institution then for men, heartily endorsed this concept for what would become their sister institution.[3]

By the early 1960s, the college was fully engaged in the secular world, while its Catholic ties sheltered it from many of the day's controversies. Trinity College in those days was a place where young women could flourish, protected from the influences of society and even men. The yearbooks from that era show young, Caucasian, Catholic women, partaking in traditional academics and activities. They were taught both by nuns in severe habits and by lay teachers, with Catholicism at the root of their studies.

But the Catholic world around them was being stretched in many ways. Democrat John F. Kennedy, Nancy's former dinner partner, was elected president during her time at college, the first Roman Catholic to hold the office. He urged the nation to ask "what you can do for your country," inspiring an entire generation to public service.[4]

In the 1961 yearbook, "The Trinologue," a picture shows Nancy and fellow classmates campaigning for Kennedy in 1960. She's holding a sign with another student, looking enthusiastic and engaged. It's probably safe to say that she was the only one in the picture who had actually had dinner with the candidate.

Interestingly, the campus was as divided as the nation about the election of 1960. Another picture shows an equally enthusiastic group of students campaigning for Kennedy's opponent, Richard M. Nixon, the Republican candidate.

But Kennedy won. The impact of that victory was felt across the nation, particularly by young people, as he was only 43 years old at the time and projected an image of youth and vigor (or "vigah," as he pronounced it in his broad Boston accent). Nowhere was that victory felt more deeply than among the young Catholics of the nation, who hung Kennedy's picture proudly next to pictures of the Pope.

Years later, the memory of Kennedy continued to inspire Nancy.

In a televised address responding to President George W. Bush's State of the Union Speech on January 21, 2004, Pelosi invoked Kennedy.

"Forty-three years ago today, as a college student standing in the freezing cold outside this Capitol building, I heard President Kennedy issue this challenge in his inaugural address: 'My fellow citizens of the world,' he said, 'ask not what America will do for you, but what working together we can do for the freedom of man,'" she said in calling her party to work together for the same freedoms.[5]

And at the same time as Kennedy's campaign and election, the Catholic Church was being radically remade to respond to modern times by Pope John XXIII and by his successor, Pope Paul VI, who carried on John's work, and by the advent of the more liberal Second Ecumenical Vatican Council, or "Vatican II."

Gone was the Latin Mass, which had stood for centuries as the centerpiece of the Catholic ritual—replaced with services in the vernacular of the country in which the services were held. For Americans, that meant Mass in English.

The church moved away from the position it had taken as the perfect society or the kingdom of God on earth and described itself as a sacrament to the world instead. It also began to accept other religions as legitimate and began to condemn anti-Semitism. Lay people, not priests or nuns, were given more authority in the church, as well. And the church began to put more emphasis on human dignity and religious liberty.[6]

All of these changes had a tremendous influence on Nancy, as she navigated through the path of her college education and activities. She majored in political science, reflecting her upbringing. Her senior photo shows a demure face in profile, with the legend underneath "Solemn she is rarely seen, yet thoughts and deep are there."

Not surprisingly, she was a member of the International Relations Club and the Political Affairs Club, as well as the Dramatic Society and the French Club. She also participated for one year in an organization called the "Wekies," which raised money for Catholic missions abroad. It was a precursor for a talent that would surface many years later—the ability to raise money for political causes.

Along with her studies, these influences of the world around her made a great impression on Nancy.

"It was a start of a very important time for Catholics in this country. It was a time of optimism and hope. Inspired by President Kennedy, young, idealistic Americans joined the Peace Corps.... And in our Church, our beloved Pope John XXIII called for a great renewal of the Church in the modern world, a renewal that would become Vatican II. He reinvigorated the Church with a new openness while remaining true to the unshakable foundations of our faith, and he intensified our faith in God and in each other. He would have been open to the Sisters of Notre Dame," she said.

"Trinity College was the perfect place to be at that exciting time. It provided the serenity and the teaching to appreciate the gift of faith and the conviction that we all contain a spark of divinity, and our beautiful chapel was a magnet for us."[7]

Pelosi valued her women's college experience at Trinity College. In an interview with the Trinity magazine, she reflected on her college years:

"I loved Trinity College. It was an absolute joy to go there. We were in Washington, D.C., so I was active with the College Democrats. All of us, we felt very nurtured at Trinity. Our friendships are stronger today than they were then. My best friends from Trinity are still my best friends," she said.[8]

She kept those friends for life. One of them, Martha Dodd Buonanno, remembers meeting Nancy as a freshman at Trinity. Buonanno was from Connecticut, and on her drive south through Maryland to Trinity, in Washington, D.C., she passed many billboards advertising a "Tommy D'Alesandro," who was running for Senate.

As Buonanno tells the story, she first met Nancy at a freshman func-
tion in 1958 where they were all required to wear nametags. Seeing
the "D'Alesandro" tag on Nancy, she asked if Nancy was related to the
"D'Alesandro" who was on all those billboards as a Senate candidate (unsuccessful, as it turned out). A bit puzzled, Nancy asked why she wanted
to know that. Well, Buonanno said, my father is running for Senate, too.
It turned out Buonanno's father was Thomas Dodd, who represented
Connecticut in the Senate for eight years, from 1958 to 1970.

From that introduction through their political fathers, Nancy and Martha became fast and lifelong friends.

"We really wanted to be freshmen in college, not 'daughters of,'" Buonanno remembered. "I went 350 miles away. She wanted to get away, but
still got involved in politics."[9]

Both majored in political science. Buonanno recalled Pelosi as a "bril-
liant" student who "didn't study, she just got it."[10]

While at Trinity, Nancy met another person who would be with her
for most of her life, her future husband, Paul Pelosi. Paul was a tall, handsome man from San Francisco, who was a student at Georgetown University in Washington when Nancy met him.

Paul Pelosi came from a strong Catholic family in San Francisco, where
his father was a wholesale druggist. He, too, had attended Catholic schools
growing up and went to high school at St. Ignatius in San Francisco. He
came East at first to attend Malvern Preparatory School in Pennsylvania
and then to college at Georgetown.[11]

Nancy and Paul first crossed paths when they both took a summer
school class at Georgetown's School for Foreign Service called "The History of Africa, South of the Sahara," taught by the legendary Professor
Carroll Quigley.[12]

That was the same Prof. Quigley who had inspired another young
Georgetown student who went on to become president of the United
States, Bill Clinton. Clinton referred to Quigley in his address on July 16,
1992, in accepting the Democratic nomination for president.

"As a teenager, I heard John Kennedy's summons to citizenship," Clinton said. "And then, as a student at Georgetown, I head that call clarified
by a professor named Caroll Quigley, who said to us that America was the
greatest Nation in history because our people had always believed in two
things—that tomorrow can be better than today and that every one of us
has a personal moral responsibility to make it so."[13]

After meeting in Quigley's class, Paul Pelosi asked the young Nancy
D'Alesandro out and apparently pursued her when she was somewhat
indifferent at first.

Asked in an interview in 1984 what had struck him about Nancy, he said it was an easy question.

"She was just special. She was very bright, had a terrific personality. She had a very uncanny way about her. She was also pretty. So it was easy, very easy."[14]

He was her first serious boyfriend, and soon they were inseparable. They were beginning to be a couple in their friends' minds. They often double-dated with Martha and her boyfriend, Bernard Buonanno, who later became her husband.

Marriage was looming. But first, Paul had to survive the D'Alesandro family's test.

"We always spent our summers down to Ocean City," said Tommy D'Alesandro, Nancy's brother. "She had to take Paul down to Ocean City to go through the gauntlet and meet all of us and meet our father. [Paul] was a classy guy."[15]

After getting the degree in political science, and with her experience both with the Political Club and International Relations Club at Trinity, along with her family political connections, Nancy landed a summer internship job with Sen. Daniel Brewster, a Maryland Democrat. Also interning in the Brewster office that summer was another young, ambitious embryonic politician, Steny Hoyer. Like Nancy, Hoyer had deep roots in Maryland and a lot of ambition.

Hoyer and Pelosi would meet again—in the House of Representatives—and for a time, they would be rivals. Eventually, they would work together, and Hoyer served as Pelosi's second in command in the House, as Majority Leader, when she first became Speaker.

But, back in the 1960s, Nancy got a taste of the different treatment afforded men and women on Capitol Hill. That was something that would irk her for decades.

Hoyer "worked directly for me and helped me with a number of different projects," Brewster said in an interview more than 40 years later. Pelosi was a receptionist—or, as Brewster put it, "an excellent front person."[16]

Hoyer recalled working with Nancy in the Brewster office, and particularly that in her role as receptionist, Nancy always made people feel "welcomed, listened to, attentive. Nancy was all that. I'm sure that nobody who came in didn't go away with a good feeling of how gracious she was and how welcoming she was."

Hoyer also noted that Nancy came from a very prominent political family in Baltimore and said that the young people in the office knew she was a "big wheel because of her family."[17]

Hoyer also remembered that Paul Pelosi came around quite often and that the young people in the office knew that Paul and Nancy were dating.

Paul and Nancy were married September 7, 1963, a year after they both graduated from their two institutions. As much of a stretch as it was for Nancy's Baltimore family to contemplate her marrying someone from so far away, it apparently was the same for Paul's family. Their engagement announcement in the *San Francisco Chronicle* at the time noted that Paul Pelosi "will marry in the East," as if it were some exotic locale. The engagement notice mentioned that Paul was working on a graduate degree at New York University, where they would move after marrying.[18]

Their wedding was a lavish affair, befitting the Baltimore family's prominence. Nancy had a gown of Alencon lace and a full chapel-length train. Ronald Pelosi was his brother's best man, and Nancy had her brother's wives and her friends as attendants.[19]

Nancy and her friend Martha Dodd Buonanno were married two weeks apart. The newly wed Buonannos were in the newly married Pelosi's apartment in November 1963, in the days after President Kennedy was shot and killed. Martha Dodd Buonanno remembered they were all watching television when Jack Ruby of Dallas shot the accused assassin, Lee Harvey Oswald, on live television. "We were down in their apartment in New York after Kennedy was assassinated. We saw Jack Ruby kill Oswald," she said.[20]

The Pelosis stayed in New York for a few years and then moved to San Francisco, Paul's hometown, where Nancy would strike out on her own politically. But, first, she decided to have a family.

NOTES

1. "Pelosi Carrying on Political Tradition," *San Jose Mercury News*, October 2, 2006, p. 1.

2. Ibid.

3. *The Catholic Encyclopedia*, Vol. XV (New York: Robert Appleton Company, 1912).

4. John F. Kennedy, Inaugural Address, January 20, 1961, Washington, D.C.

5. Pelosi, televised address to the nation, January 21, 2004, Democratic response to the president's State of the Union speech.

6. Kevin M. Vander Schel, "The Influence of the Second Vatican Council," Boston Collaborative Encyclopedia of Modern Western Theology (2005). Available online at http://people.bu.edu/wwildman/WeirdWildWeb/courses/mwt/dictionary/mwt_themes_900_vatican2.htm.

7. Speech to women's convocation, Trinity University, September 25, 2003.

8. Peggy Lewis, *Trinity* Magazine, "Profile: Nancy Pelosi '62 House Democratic Leader," Fall 2003.

9. Martha Buonanno, interview with author, Providence, R.I., December 2, 2007.

10. Ibid.

11. "Paul Pelosi Will Marry in the East," *San Francisco Chronicle,* May 27, 1963, p. 20.

12. Pelosi, speech to the Georgetown University School of Foreign Service Commencement, Washington, D.C., May 18, 2002.

13. Bill Clinton, speech to the Democratic National Convention, New York, July 16, 1992.

14. Jane Ferrell, "A Highly Conventional Democrat," *California Living Magazine,* January 15, 1984, pp. 8–12.

15. Thomas D'Alesandro III, interview with author, Baltimore, August 14, 2007.

16. Emily Haile, "Former U.S. Senator Recalls Hoyer, Pelosi in Bygone Days," Capital News Service, November 15, 2006.

17. Steny Hoyer, interview with author, Washington, D.C., October 24, 2007.

18. "Paul Pelosi Will Marry in the East," *San Francisco Chronicle,* May 27, 1963.

19. "Weddings," *San Francisco Chronicle,* September 18, 1963.

20. Martha Buonanno, interview with author, Providence, R.I., December 2, 2007.

Chapter 3

CHILDREN AND VOLUNTEERING

After her marriage in 1963, Nancy D'Alesandro Pelosi, the girl who had never lived more than 40 miles from her Baltimore home, found herself first in New York with her new husband for five years and then in San Francisco, his hometown. Not only was she far away from friends and family, she started immediately to have a family of her own. By her own admission, she was pregnant for much of the 1960s—having five children in six years and one week, beginning with Nancy Corinne in 1964. Her first four children were born in New York; after Nancy Corinne came Christine, in May 1966, Jacqueline, in July 1967, and Paul Jr., in January 1969. The last, Alexandra, was born in October 1970 in San Francisco.

Other than being a wife and mother, Pelosi didn't really have career ambitions at this point in her life. She has said she didn't really know what she wanted to do after graduation. "I was always around politics, but I knew one thing: I never wanted to run for public office," she told a group of schoolchildren in 2007 who visited her in the Speaker's Office for "Take Your Child to Work Day." The irony of that comment, given the locale, was not lost on the kids.

Her college degree was in political science, which made sense given her background, but she was concentrating on being a mother and homemaker. Yet politics—the family business—was never far away. She started emulating her mother in the "woman behind the scenes" role. But, in her generation, she wasn't supporting a husband like her mother did (Paul had never had political ambitions); she was supporting a party and its causes.

Along the way, she was continually caring for her kids because she never could find much in the way of babysitters, as the challenge of all those kids was far too daunting.

"When you raise five children born six years apart, you do most of the work yourself. You can't attract a good deal of people to help out," she said. "It trains you to anticipate, to be organized and to be flexible."[1]

She brought the kids to political events, stuffed envelopes and rang doorbells with them tagging along. She did what she knew best—she volunteered for the Democratic Party and for political races. It was what her mother had done as the head of the Democratic Club in Little Italy.

"I have never not participated in a campaign," she said during her first run for Congress, "no matter how little my babies were, if I was wheeling them in a carriage or carrying them in my stomach."

Pelosi was lucky in that her husband, Paul, was making a handsome living as a real estate developer and investor in San Francisco. It allowed her the freedom to stay home, raise children, and do volunteer work. She never had to work outside the home, and many times during her career she marveled at how women with both careers and children managed both.

"I had five children in six years, so that was a challenge in and of itself. But I was very fortunate. My husband was a very cooperative spouse and we, that's what we did—we raised our children. We had to work, of course, but our focus was on our children, and my focus was on them until they were of such an age where I could do other things. But what I learned is that no matter what your economic situation, you still need to pay a great deal of attention to your children as you're raising them," she said. "I simply have complete awe for women who are holding down jobs and raising a family. They have my complete and utter respect."[2]

As a young mother, Pelosi was something of a drill sergeant.

"She was extremely well-organized," recalled her daughter, Christine, second of the five Pelosi children. "She was a sequencer. There would be a food assembly line for lunch. There would be ten pieces of bread and five drinks to take. You would make your own sandwich, grab an apple and a snack and a drink, put it in a bag and go to school."[3]

Every evening, a similar routine ensued.

"Someone would set the table, someone would help cook, someone would clean up. Someone would put the dishes on the table for the next morning's breakfast. We weren't starting from scratch every day," Christine Pelosi said. "Every night, the Catholic school uniforms were pressed and shoes were shined. At night it was wash, teeth, uniform, homework, say prayers and go to bed."[4]

Pelosi was the epitome of the busy mom—driving her five children to school and to all of their activities in a red Wagoneer.

"She was always the class mom, baking cookies," said daughter Alexandra, the youngest of the children, born in 1970. "She would go to all our games."[5]

She also drove on class field trips to the Old Mint in San Francisco, brought cupcakes to school, and sewed her children's Halloween costumes. Alexandra held onto one special costume, a pink angel with silver wings.[6]

Paul and Nancy Pelosi were by all accounts happy being parents; that's what they wanted to do. But they weren't pushovers. When it came time for homework, Pelosi instilled her children with respect for themselves and responsibility.

"Proper preparation prevents poor performance," Christine recalled her saying. She said her mom instilled in the kids that if they had a test, they would feel better about themselves if they studied and were prepared.

And she never took sides in the kids' spats.

"She would say, 'if you play rough, you get hurt,'" according to Christine Pelosi. "'Throw a punch, take a punch.'"[7]

When there were different interpretations of what constituted bedtime, she would set boundaries and enforce them.

If one child was telling on another, she would counsel them not to be a tattletale.

"I'm not taking any complaints; let's have some cooperation," she said then.

But if there was evidence that one child had transgressed, that child would be disciplined, but out of view of the others, so that they could take no satisfaction from their sibling's punishment.

BEGINNINGS OF ACTIVISM

All of the balancing was interwoven into her beginnings as a Democratic activist in San Francisco. Previously in politics, she had been known as the D'Alesandro girl from Baltimore, but now, 3,000 miles away, she was doing it on her own, as "Nancy Pelosi."

She began having fundraising meetings in her Presidio Terrace home along with her volunteer work. In 1975, she was appointed to the city's Library Commission, a volunteer job, but one that was overseen by Mayor Joseph Alioto, and that brought her a bit further into the political arena. She was also a "consultant' to the National Conference of Mayors, another volunteer political-type job. She also worked on campaigns of Leo McCarthy, who was then in the California Assembly and who would turn out to be a mentor for Pelosi, and for future California Gov. Jerry Brown.

The 1960s and early 1970s were a turbulent time in the nation, with the civil rights movement and protests against the Vietnam War in the forefront. There is little evidence that Pelosi was directly involved in either issue, though they certainly permeated the politics of the time.

In the 1960s and 1970s, San Francisco became a magnet for hippies, young people who dropped out of school or other society and sought more freedom and created their own communities. They listened to psychedelic rock music, created colorful artworks based on music or drug experiences, embraced the sexual revolution, and sometimes used marijuana or other drugs like LSD. In 1967, the San Francisco "be-in" brought thousands of young people to the city, and the "Summer of Love" started there and spread to the entire West Coast.

Pelosi was involved with none of it. She was a young mother of five children, all of whom were enrolled in parochial schools, far away from the hippie culture.

Moving into the 1970s and 1980s, San Francisco became a center of the homosexual or "gay" rights movement, culminating with the election of Harvey Milk, who was openly gay, to the city's Board of Supervisors, and his assassination, along with Mayor George Moscone, in 1978.

The gay rights movement became a much bigger part of the political life in San Francisco, as many gay people moved into the Democratic Party. Pelosi worked with the gay members of the party in an inclusive manner.

Her home was a jumble of politics and family, recalled Agar Jaicks, a political friend of Pelosi's for more than 30 years. Jaicks, a television director and producer, became involved in the civil rights movement in the 1950s and 1960s and was eventually elected to the San Francisco Democratic County Central Committee.

Going to meetings and events at Pelosi's home meant getting a window into her balancing act of home and family, Jaicks recalled.

"The children were always there," Jaicks said "They had five of them. I didn't notice it, but she was totally aware of what was going on with her kids and carrying on a conversation with me at the same time. She'd say, 'I can't stand it, they are always fighting,'"[8]

The home was comfortable, but not showy. It was big enough to hold public events, fundraisers, coffees, and meetings, and big enough to hold the family.

"It wasn't manicured," Jaicks said. "Not some place where you'd be afraid to sit in 'that' chair."[9]

Sam Lauter, who grew up with the Pelosi kids and three siblings of his own on Presidio Terrace, remembers running in an out of each other's houses—just as Nancy had years before in Little Italy. "There were a lot of kids in the neighborhood, adding five more was just five more. The doors tended to be unlocked. The Pelosis had better chocolate chip cookies than we did and I tended to go over and get the cookies.

"They would come over to our house for Passover seders and we would go to their house for Christmas," Lauter remembered.[10]

Lauter's mother, Naomi, and Pelosi became close friends, and they found that, in addition to having all those kids, they had Democratic politics in common, according to Sam Lauter. They volunteered together, and they "volunteered" the kids.

"We had envelope-stuffing parties at both houses," Lauter said. "All the kids."[11]

Naomi Lauter marveled at her neighbor's organizational skills.

"She brought the neighborhood together; she was an organizer," Naomi Lauter remembered. At Democratic events in the Pelosi home, the children would pass hors d'oeuvres and would help out.

She organized the neighborhood to back one of her early political mentors, then Lt. Gov. Leo McCarthy. "She had a 'progressive dinner' in the neighborhood for Leo McCarthy," Naomi Lauter said. "Which meant she aligned her neighbors to join in support of Leo, who she adored."[12]

There was plenty of food, none of it catered. She would make things ahead of time or buy prepared foods and serve them herself, along with the kids.

Paul Pelosi supported her every step of the way. Some nights, she would feed the children, bathe them, put them to bed, and then sit down with Paul and have a late dinner.

He supported her Democratic Party work in those years, even though he was not as active as she was in the party work.

Nancy Pelosi also became involved with then Rep. Philip Burton of San Francisco, who became another mentor and who would also figure very significantly in her later political life. John Burton, Philip's brother and himself a former member of Congress and of the California Assembly, remembers being "duly unimpressed" with Pelosi in the early 1970s, but not because of anything she herself had done. Her brother-in-law, Ron Pelosi, had been a member of the San Francisco Board of Supervisors and, as John Burton put it, "a member of the other Democratic clique" in town. That put Nancy Pelosi in the "other clique," as well, at least in Burton's eyes, at first.[13]

But that soon changed, particularly when virtually all of the Democratic Party members in the state came behind Gov. Jerry Brown. Burton recalled an event for Brown, in which Nancy Pelosi appeared in a "lime green jumpsuit"—even then she was memorable for her wardrobe.[14]

GOV. JERRY BROWN

In 1976, Pelosi found a way to use her old Baltimore family and political connections to help out a Californian, effectively tying the two parts of her political life together. Then California Gov. Jerry Brown was running for president, and he asked her to help run his primary campaign in Maryland. Her work proved so helpful that Brown upset the front-runner, Georgia Gov. Jimmy Carter, and won the Maryland primary. Carter, of course, went on to win the Democratic nomination and then the presidency, but Pelosi's political organizing credentials remained untarnished.

She used the old-fashioned coalition building and "machine" politics championed by her father and brother, who was then mayor of Baltimore. Pelosi came into Baltimore and arranged a meeting with her father, her brother Tommy, the mayor, and other "progressives" in the Maryland Democratic Party. They got together and went to court Marvin Mandel, who was then the governor of Maryland and a very powerful figure in Maryland politics.

There was no love lost between Mandel and Carter, stemming from Carter's opposition to Mandel when Mandel was running for chairman of the Democratic Governor's Conference. So Mandel was looking for an alternative to Carter, and Pelosi presented him with Jerry Brown.

"It was the first and only time that the old guard and the new wing got together in a political campaign," remembered Frank DeFilippo, who was Mandel's press secretary and chief of staff. "Marvin got all the old-line political bosses together and elected officials in the Hilton in Baltimore and said he didn't have any 'walking around money [payoffs] for this one, but I'll take care of you next time.' And they delivered the state for Jerry Brown," DeFilippo said.[15]

While it was Mandel and the Maryland Democratic political machine that delivered the state for Brown, it could not have been pulled off without Pelosi's bringing them together and making the pitch for Brown. She sold the old-line officials on the liberal governor from California and set the wheels in motion.

But when Carter eventually won the nomination, she went to work fundraising for him and volunteering for Democratic elections in 1976.

After the election, Brown rewarded her in 1977 by making her chairwoman of the Northern California Democratic Party. In that position, which she held until 1981, she continued her volunteer work, all the while balancing the family.

She shared office space with Jaicks' organization, the San Francisco County Central Committee, renting him some unused space in her office suite.

"She was very warm and friendly," Jaicks said. "She would get phone calls from the children, and she would solve problems on the telephone. I can remember a phone call she got and told them to stop fighting and then asked, 'What have you done about your homework?' And she would talk to them and then get back to her business as chair of the Northern California Democratic Party."

She was beginning to make a name for herself outside Baltimore and California, as well, and was beginning to be recognized by the Democratic Party nationwide. When President Jimmy Carter was looking for a delegation to send to Italy in December 1980 to study relief efforts for a devastating earthquake there, Pelosi was named to the eight-member group—all Italian Americans. The delegates included then-New York Gov. Mario Cuomo and Rep. Geraldine Ferraro, along with several other members of the House beside whom Pelosi would one day serve. "We went to Italy on Air Force One," Cuomo remembered. He said Pelosi was a "beautiful person" and dedicated to helping the people of Italy recover from the quake, which had, among other things, collapsed a church, killing about 100 people.[16]

Back in the United States, Ronald Reagan beat Jimmy Carter for the presidency in 1980, dealing a huge blow to the Democratic Party, since it was very unusual for a sitting president to be defeated for a second term. Reagan's victory was helped by the Iran hostage crisis, in which American hostages were held in Iran for 444 days, from November 4, 1979, to January 20, 1981. Carter authorized a rescue mission, which failed spectacularly, leading to dissatisfaction with him as president.

Helping to pick up the pieces of the wreckage of the party was Nancy Pelosi, who had parlayed the Northern California Democratic Party job into election as the State of California chairwoman of the Democratic Party. She continued to draw attention as a dynamite fundraiser and Democratic advocate, although she got into a bit of controversy over a 1982 state mailer that misrepresented the party's position on two ballot measures—one on gun control and one urging some voters in the south to support a Republican. She didn't have much to do with the mailers—they were advanced by Assembly Speaker Willie Brown—but Democratic Party money was used to pay for them.[17]

She also was very involved in Leo McCarthy's campaign for lieutenant governor in 1982. McCarthy paid her back with compliments that helped her later when she was the one running for office.

"She worked on legislation in a very direct and influential way," Leo McCarthy said in 1987, when he was California's lieutenant governor and Pelosi was first running for Congress. "On Coastal Commission legislation and nuclear plant safety laws, in particular, she generated letters and made personal visits to legislators. She also did lots of fund-raising and didn't hesitate to call a legislator who she'd helped."[18]

As state party chairwoman, Pelosi worked tirelessly for Democratic causes, trying to rally the party after the devastating blow of the Reagan win in 1980. But, at the same time, family came first. She always tried to be home by 3 P.M., when the kids came home from school, except when she was attending party meetings in other parts of the country.

She moved up in Democratic politics nationally, taking some party posts along with her chairmanship of the state party, and became involved in delegate selection for the 1984 Democratic Convention.

At that point, she and her fellow San Franciscan Democrats decided to try to lure the party's convention to the "City by the Bay." She worked hard to make the city an attractive one to party leaders, hosting a series of events—some at her home—that helped attract tens of thousands of volunteers.

Her job, she explained at the time, was "to portray San Francisco as an all-American, family-oriented city."[19] That picture clashed with the ideas of some members of the African American community, who felt as though problems in the inner city of San Francisco were being papered over in an effort to lure the Democrats. Nonetheless, Pelosi's efforts were successful. Pelosi recruited 10,000 volunteers to help the city put on the convention, she raised $2.5 million in private donations to help underwrite it, and it was a success.

The convention in San Francisco made history, particularly in that it catapulted then New York Gov. Mario Cuomo on the national stage with his awe-inspiring keynote speech and in that it featured the nomination of then Rep. Geraldine Ferraro as the first woman vice presidential candidate, running with the Democratic presidential nominee, Walter Mondale.

Ferraro and Cuomo never forgot it.

Cuomo said that Pelosi had, along with Mondale and several others, encouraged him to make the keynote address at the convention—something he initially had resisted. But they persisted, and he agreed to do it. "Nancy Pelosi was helpful, without even knowing it," Cuomo said. "She was helpful to me from the beginning of my career in 1983."[20] The result was one of the most memorable convention speeches in history, in which Cuomo invoked his immigrant parents, who worked long hours in a small grocery store so that their son could live the American dream. "I saw him once literally bleed from the bottoms of his feet," Cuomo said, speaking of his father, "a man who taught me all I needed to know about faith and hard work by the simple eloquence of his example."

"I ask you, ladies and gentlemen, brothers and sisters—for the good of all of us, for the love of this great nation, for the family of America, for the love of God. Please make this nation remember how futures are built," said Cuomo, in a speech that catapulted him to the national political stage.[21]

Because of that speech and because of Pelosi's work and the work of many others, the Democratic Party left the convention united and committed in a way that few believed it could have been in light of President Ronald Reagan's strength in running for re-election. Reagan won anyway, handily, but the Democrats, instead of being demoralized, were at the very least together in defeat.

NATIONAL PARTY CANDIDATE

Pelosi's work at the convention had brought her solidly into national Democratic circles, and, at the urging of Cuomo and others, she ran for chair of the Democratic National Committee.

The leading candidate was Paul Kirk, a party activist close to Sen. Edward Kennedy of Massachusetts. Nevertheless, she threw herself into that race. She held a major Capitol Hill party for 150 political professionals and staged a fundraiser in San Francisco to underwrite her budget of $100,000 for the campaign. She almost pulled it off, but not quite.

In the end, she lost to Kirk, in a bruising race in which her slim national credentials were attacked, particularly by unions. Some of them suggested she was an "airhead," a not-very-bright homemaker who was in over her head. The criticism stung, and Pelosi got her first taste of how bruising the political world could be.

For the first time, Pelosi became combative. Gone was the smooth fundraiser and political hostess. Now, she was beginning to show her Baltimore Democratic machine roots. She accused officials of the AFL-CIO union umbrella organization of using sexist attacks to weaken her candidacy.

"They use some of the language of the day: 'She's an airhead,'" she told the *New York Times*. She singled out John Perkins, chairman of the

A.F.L.-C.I.O.'s committee on political education, as pushing an "anti-woman line."[22]

The unions denied it, but for the first time, Pelosi had broken out of the traditional "women's role" in party politics of being behind the scenes and confronted an attitude about her gender that had dogged other female politicians both before and after her.

"It is clear to me that any of you felt that the wrong message would go out if a woman was elected chairman," Pelosi told the party, and she insisted that it was fear of alienating white males that led to her defeat.[23]

Cuomo, for his part, gave interviews saying that he had been disappointed by suggestions that Pelosi might not be a good choice to lead the party because she was a woman and a Roman Catholic.[24]

It didn't help. She lost the election. The attacks, however, made her stronger and probably better able to fend off similar barrages later in her political life.

Following her unsuccessful race for party chair, she became the major fundraiser for the Democratic Senatorial Campaign Committee, the group that works to elect Democrats to the Senate. In 1986, with then Sen. George Mitchell, D-Maine, at the helm, the committee elected enough Democrats to take the majority in the Senate and make Mitchell Senate Majority Leader.

He credits Pelosi with being an expert fundraiser whose efforts paid off. "Recruiting Nancy was one of the best things I did as Chairman of the DSCC," Mitchell said. "She was terrific. My general recollection is that she was extremely helpful to all of our candidates."[25]

If the numbers are any indication, "extremely helpful" is an understatement. The Democratic Senatorial Campaign Committee raised $13.4 million in that election cycle, far eclipsing the previous record of $8.9 million and the largest amount ever raised by the committee. It was the first really big fundraising total for the Democrats in the Senate, allowing them to play in the same financial ballpark with the Republicans, who had always raised more money.

After that success, Pelosi was honored by those senators for being the "single most important individual responsible for winning the Senate in 1986."

Pelosi was emerging as a real player, but still behind the scenes, never as a candidate. "I don't want to run for anything," she said. "What I like to do is support a good candidate and involve people in the political process."[26]

Then came the events that would change her life.

NOTES

1. Mark Z. Barabak, "Triumph of the 'Airhead,'" *Los Angeles Times Magazine*, January 26, 2003, p. 12.

2. Chelsea Lollar, "House Speaker Nancy Pelosi; Children Are Inspiration for the First Woman Speaker," interview, *Scholastic News*, March 6, 2007.

3. Christine Pelosi, interview with author, December 12, 2006.

4. Ibid.

5. Bob Dart, "Political Aftershock: Nancy Pelosi," *Atlanta Journal-Constitution*, November 9, 2006, p. 1.

6. Mark Z. Barabak, "Triumph of the 'Airhead,'" *Los Angeles Times* Magazine, January 26, 2003, p. 12.

7. Christine Pelosi, interview with author, December 12, 2006.

8. Agar Jaicks, interview with author, October 18, 2007.

9. Ibid.

10. Sam Lauter, interview with author, October 26, 2007.

11. Ibid.

12. Naomi Lauter, interview with author, San Francisco, Calif., November 5, 2007.

13. John Burton, interview with author, San Francisco, Calif., November 9, 2007.

14. Ibid.

15. Frank DeFilippo, interview with author, Baltimore, Md., October 22, 2007.

16. Mario Cuomo, interview with author, New York, N.Y., October 25, 2007.

17. "Demo Bid Reported to Back Either Side of Gun Initiative," *San Francisco Chronicle*, November 13, 1982.

18. Jerry Roberts, "Washington Insider Wants to Put Her Connections to Work for S.F.," *San Francisco Chronicle*, March 23, 1987, p. 4.

19. Ibid.

20. Mario Cuomo, interview with author, New York, N.Y., October 25, 2007.

21. Mario Cuomo, speech to Democratic National Convention, San Francisco, Calif., July 16, 1984.

22. Howell Raines, "Union Accused of Sexism in Race to Lead Democrats," *New York Times*, January 29, 1985, p. B5.

23. David Johnson, "Party Picked Old Path, Pelosi Says," *San Francisco Examiner*, February 3, 1985.

24. Howell Raines," Union Accused of Sexism in Race to Lead Democrats," *New York Times*, January 29, 1985, p. B5.

25. George Mitchell, e-mail interview with author, October 30, 2007.

26. Jane Ferrell, "A Highly Conventional Democrat," *California Living Magazine*, January 15, 1984, pp. 9–12.

Chapter 4

RUNNING FOR OFFICE

In the 1960s, 1970s, and 1980s, arguably the most powerful and influential politician from California was Phil Burton. Burton was a wild man, an unrestrained liberal who moved from grassroots campaigns to the California statehouse and finally to Congress, where he served from 1964 to 1983. He took many budding politicians under his wing, including Nancy Pelosi and Rep. George Miller of California, who would become a key Pelosi confidante in later years.

Burton's achievements included the groundbreaking "black lung" law to provide assistance to miners who were afflicted with the deadly black lung disease as a result of years spent underground surrounded by coal dust. He also championed the Supplemental Security Income government program for the aged, blind, and disabled. And he helped secure America's extensive national park system. Burton's failures were equally dramatic: In 1976, at the height of his power, he lost, by one vote, the chance to become House Majority Leader, a post Pelosi would one day attain.[1]

Burton died unexpectedly of a ruptured aorta in 1983 and was succeeded in Congress by his wife, Sala, a Polish-born immigrant, who was as smooth as Phil was rough, but just as tough.

She ascended to some of the same positions that her husband had held in Congress and was an influential member of the House Rules Committee, which sets procedure for the House. She got along well in the House, as members who had only known her as Phil's wife found that she, too, had great political instincts and the ability to work within the system to achieve her goals.

But, in 1986, she too, became deathly ill. Colon cancer would prevent her from taking the oath of office in person for the next Congress that January, and she knew she did not have much time to live.

As she lay dying in Washington, D.C., she summoned Nancy Pelosi to her bedside to ask if Pelosi would run for her seat. Would she like the job and its 3,000-mile commute between San Francisco and Washington? Pelosi demurred, refusing to articulate what everyone in the room already knew—that the frail and wasted Sala Burton was not going to survive— and instead murmured something about how Burton would be all right. But finally, according to those who were in the room, including Agar Jaicks, Pelosi agreed and said she would be honored to follow Sala Burton in Congress.[2]

Jaicks then called John Burton to report that Sala, his sister-in-law, wanted Nancy to run for the seat. Burton initially thought Jaicks meant Nancy Walker, a member of the San Francisco Board of Supervisors. But, no, it was Nancy Pelosi she wanted.[3]

Still unconvinced, John Burton met Pelosi in a cocktail lounge in the Bank of America Building in downtown San Francisco to feel her out. "She said, 'if you think my running would become an embarrassment to you or your family, I won't run,'" Burton recalled. "I said I didn't say that, I said if Sala wants you, it's fine with me.'"

So Burton went to Washington, where Sala was in the hospital. "And Sala, she was a fairly zaftig woman, and she was down to this," Burton said, holding his hands about six inches apart.

"And she [Sala] went through this whole litany. She laid out every attribute, except fate, that would lead Nancy to be Speaker. She's smart, she's tough, she's operational, and she's good on everything we care about," Burton said, "Operational means you know what it takes to run campaigns and win campaigns."[4]

Burton came back to San Francisco from that meeting, figuring that his sister-in-law didn't have much time to live. He held a press conference, saying that Sala Burton wanted Nancy Pelosi to run for the seat, putting the imprimatur of the Burton family on the Pelosi candidacy. And after that, he campaigned with her day and night, re-emphasizing the Burton connection for the voters.

Pelosi, at age 47, having never held elective office before, was suddenly Sala Burton's heir apparent. Burton's death led to a raucous 14-candidate special election in June 1987. Pelosi was portrayed as something of a dilettante, a "mere" housewife, or an "airhead," who had never run for anything before. One rival dubbed her "the party girl of the Party."

It wasn't very flattering, but Pelosi was determined, once in the race, to see it through. Her children also were growing up, giving her more freedom. The youngest, Alexandra, was in high school, and the oldest was 22. Having spent the better part of two decades raising them, she suddenly had more time for herself. She got into the race with all of her energy. She had taken a job at the public relations firm Ogilvie and Mather, but that got put on hold as she geared up for the campaign. She put all of her political skills to work.

What followed was a no-holds barred campaign that would test every one of Pelosi's political instincts. It was the first time in decades that the seat was going to be held by someone other than a member of the Burton family, and many San Francisco politicians thought that it was either their turn to go to Congress or that the Burtons shouldn't get to pick their own successor.

In the first place, the critics were partially right: Pelosi was always behind the scenes in politics, never the candidate out front. And being the candidate herself took new a new set of skills that she had to learn as she went.

"The fact is that there is an opportunity now in Congress," she said at the time. "There are people who are willing to support me, and I have to cross that threshold from being a private person who works without fanfare to somebody who puts herself on the line."

"I'm a competitor, and if I get in this race, I'm getting in it to win. I have an incredible endorsement from Sala, and I want to make sure I do everything I can to win because she has put so much confidence in me."[5]

She had a number of things going for her as she got into the race. For example, during the 1984 convention, she made sure that a lot of different businesses in San Francisco benefited from the thousands of convention-goers, not just the big downtown hotels. The conventioneers were given information on lots of little stores and restaurants, assuring them a piece of the convention pie. They remembered.

In addition, she had a great personality, and she never forgot a name.

"When she announced, I took her all around the neighborhood," said Ed Moose, who owned a restaurant in the North Beach section of the city that was a hangout for politicians and journalists. "People out here knew very little about her Baltimore roots. She was a natural campaigner and everyone was charmed by her."[6]

But, in the beginning, there were also stumbles. She was not an articulate speaker, and she sometimes had that "deer-in-the-headlights" stare that reflected nervousness and fear, even if she didn't feel that way. She was young looking and attractive as well, which proved to be a double-edged sword.

Normally soft spoken, Pelosi adopted as her campaign slogan "A Voice That Will Be Heard." That slogan was created so that it could be interpreted in many ways. First, it rebutted the perception that she was too quiet and behind-the-scenes. Second, it invoked her ties to Democratic leaders in Congress who would presumably listen to her in ways that they would not necessarily to other ordinary congressional freshmen. And, last, it traded on her family's experience in politics, which had presumably taught her how to make her voice heard.

She announced her candidacy on February 14—Valentine's Day—that year, saying that as a member of Congress, "I will be able to put my experience and friendships in Washington to work for San Francisco."[7]

Her slogan also traded on what would later be called her "Mother of Five" voice—the commanding tone that she took with her children when they were to pay attention to her.

Most of the other candidates were members of the San Francisco Board of Supervisors, and they used that experience to attack her. But since she had a number of high-profile endorsements—from John Burton, Sala's brother-in-law; Leo McCarthy, the California lieutenant governor speaker at the time; San Francisco Mayor Dianne Feinstein; and then Sen. Alan Cranston—the election became about her, not about any of the others.

She called in all the chits. Sen. Barbara Mikulski, D-Maryland, for whom Pelosi had raised money and campaigned in her successful 1986 race for the Senate, came to help. The other senators that she knew chipped in. She ran advertising and spoke at every available event. And she raised money, amassing more than half a million dollars for the campaign—which was considered big money in those days.

But mostly, she campaigned the way she had been taught in Baltimore all those years ago—house to house, street to street, neighborhood to neighborhood. With all those candidates in the race, the constituents were divided. Michael Yaki, who was a young law clerk at the time and who would go on to be Pelosi's right-hand man, volunteered for her campaign and was sent to a Chinese-American event. He got there early and was told that his candidate's appearance had been moved up half an hour and, of course, the candidate was nowhere to be found. Turned out the group was supporting some one else and did not want to receive Pelosi at all. But Yaki, called on at the last minute to take her place, vamped for nearly half an hour until she could rush to the event and talk to the group.[8]

Pelosi also was helped by the fact that Phil Burton had had a tough race just five years earlier, forcing him to campaign hard and to ramp up his organization. The fact was that Phil Burton's campaigns had been pretty easy for most of the time that he was in Congress, but in 1982, Milton Marks, a Republican-turned-Democrat and a career politician, decided to take him on and made a real race of it. Marks outspent Burton by nearly $100,000. Marks got support from President Reagan's lieutenants, Republicans who were eager to have the powerful Burton out of Congress. While Marks declined to have Reagan administration officials campaign in a Democratic district, he was not above using the Washington connection to skewer Burton. Marks charged that Burton rarely came home from Washington, calling him a "ghost who occasionally haunts our city."

Burton won by 30,000 votes, but the race reinvigorated his on-the-ground political operation—an operation that Sala inherited and, then, Nancy Pelosi.[9]

She held that coalition together—environmentalists, labor unions, women—and added her own groundwork to the effort.

Pelosi appeared at more than 120 house parties over the course of that 60-day snap election, and when her brother Tommy flew out to inspect the ground troops, he paid her the ultimate compliment. "This," D'Alesandro said, "is how we did it in Baltimore."[10]

Ronald Reagan was president, and his policies were prevalent in the country. He won re-election in 1984, crushing the Democrats' Walter Mondale, and Democrats were looking for some clear voices in Congress.

Pelosi ran on improving education—something she knew well as a mother, although she sent her children to parochial schools, not public schools—and on opposition to the social welfare policies of President Reagan. Reagan had campaigned on getting rid of so-called welfare queens, women who, he said, had children just so they could live off welfare payments. Reagan cut the social welfare programs, much to the dismay of many Democrats who disputed his contentions.

Pelosi also was upset at what she perceived as Reagan's lack of concern over clean air and water, more government aid for the homeless, and an end to aid for the Nicaraguan "Contras," an anti-Communist rebel band in that Central American country.

A year earlier, it had been revealed that the Reagan administration had sold weapons to an avowed enemy, Iran, and used the profits to fund the Contra rebels. A full-blown scandal ensued, and many Democrats who were running for office in those years tried to use it as an example of what was wrong with Reagan and the Republicans.

Pelosi also confronted the issue of Acquired Immune Deficiency Syndrome, or AIDS, which had devastated San Francisco, particularly the homosexual community. The disease was foremost in the minds of San

Franciscans but ignored by many Americans, including President Reagan, who had only that year given a speech about it. AIDS had been observed and diagnosed for almost a decade, at that point.

The gay community in San Francisco was divided on the election. An openly gay supervisor, Harry Britt, was running in the same election as Pelosi and had laid claim to the support of the gay community. But, as surveys showed after the election, Pelosi had made substantial inroads into that politically active group.

She also got a boost from Republicans, many of whom voted for her rather than Britt or any of the other candidates. Britt actually won more votes from Democrats than Pelosi, but she appealed to a broader spectrum of voters.

Interestingly, Pelosi sent out a flyer during the election that touted her appeal across party lines to Republicans. While saying she was a "rabid, partisan Democrat" in speeches and on television, Pelosi's mailing touted her as being able to give San Francisco the "balanced representation" it deserved.[11]

"You don't go to Congress just to vote," she said at the time. "It's important to have special representation for this special district. I'm taken very seriously in Washington. I understand Congress and I know what it would take to get them to act on something."[12]

DEBATES AND BALLOTS

The campaign was symbolized by a wild candidates' debate, held in early April of that year by KQED-TV, prompting one caller to the television station to say it was "better than any Monty Python I've ever seen." In a fitting tribute, a re-run of the debate was shown opposite the late-night comedy show *Saturday Night Live*.

Before the show, one KQED producer expressed concern that the forum would be boring. He needn't have worried.

The show produced not only several shouting matches but also suggestions by some of the candidates that bombing Iran's Ayatollah Khomeini and the headquarters of Nicaragua's Sandinista government would be okay.

At the end of the show, the "Peace and Freedom" Party candidate, Ted Zuur, was hauled off by a security guard, and the fringe Democrat, an acolyte of Lyndon LaRouche, suggested that he was on a first-name basis with the Pope.

In contrast, Pelosi appeared demure and reasonable, if not particularly articulate.

On April 9, Pelosi got more votes than any other candidate, outpolling five fellow Democrats and eight other candidates, with 36 percent of the vote.

Because she did not get 50 percent of the vote or more, she was forced into a runoff with the Republicans' top vote-getter, Harriet Ross, a deputy public defender.

But since the San Francisco district was 64 percent Democratic, getting the most votes in the first election was tantamount to victory for Pelosi. Her closest opponent, Supervisor Britt, an open homosexual, got 32 percent of the vote and came within 4,000 votes of beating her. His good showing began to galvanize the gay political community in San Francisco. But Pelosi won or was runner up in all 17 neighborhoods in the congressional district, and she had all-around appeal.

A survey by the *San Francisco Examiner* at the time showed that 21 percent of homosexuals voted for Pelosi, while Britt won the votes of 23 percent of those voters who said they were heterosexuals. The newspaper also speculated that Pelosi's money and fundraising ability had made the difference.[13]

She finally won the special election on June 3, 1987, with 67 percent of the vote to 33 percent for Republican Harriet Ross.

With jubilation and excitement, Nancy Patricia D'Alesandro Pelosi was headed to Washington. But what awaited her there was far different from what she had campaigned on.

NOTES

1. John Jacobs, *A Rage for Justice: The Passion and Politics of Phillip Burton* (Berkeley: University of California Press, 1997), introduction/summary.

2. Mark Z. Barabak, "Triumph of the 'Airhead,'" *Los Angeles Times Magazine*, January 26, 2003, p. 12.

3. John Burton, interview with author, San Francisco, November 10, 2007.

4. Ibid.

5. Ruthe Stein, "A Friend, Perhaps an Heir/ Nancy Pelosi Gets Serious about Congress," *San Francisco Chronicle*, February 3, 1987, p. 1.

6. Ed Moose, interview with author, San Francisco, Nov. 10, 2007.

7. Jerry Roberts, "A Washington Insider Wants to Put Her Connections to Work for S.F.," *San Francisco Chronicle*, March 23, 1987, p. 4.

8. Michael Yaki, interview with author, San Francisco, November 10, 2007.

9. Larry D. Hatfield, "Political Icon in S.F. Dies: Milton Marks, 1920–1998," *San Francisco Examiner*, December 4, 1998, section A.

10. Mark Z. Barabak, "Triumph of the 'Airhead,'" *Los Angeles Times Magazine*, January 26, 2003, p. 12.

11. Jerry Roberts, "'Rabid' Demo Pelosi Tries for GOP Votes," *San Francisco Chronicle*, April 4, 1987, p. 4.

12. Mark Z. Barabak, "Triumph of the 'Airhead,'" *Los Angeles Times Magazine*, January 26, 2003, p. 12.

13. Robert Lindsey, "House Race in West Goes to Runoff," *New York Times*, April 9, 1987, p. A1.

Chapter 5

ROOKIE REPRESENTATIVE

On June 11, 1987, Pelosi was sworn in as a United States Representative in the great House of Representatives chamber with her proud family and friends looking on. Posing for pictures with Speaker Jim Wright, D-Texas, later that day, Pelosi was surrounded by family, including her father, who by that time was ill and in a wheelchair. He would die of a heart attack two months later.

But, ironically, the woman who had campaigned on the slogan "A Voice That Will Be Heard" was told initially to keep quiet. In those days, freshmen representatives, no matter who their relatives were, were expected to stay in the background, and learn.

Speaker Wright, the man who had beaten Phil Burton by one vote for the Majority Leader's job back in 1976, in a twist of fate was the one who administered the oath to Pelosi and who initially said she shouldn't make a speech on her first day. But, under pressure from those who knew her father and brother, he relented.

"When I came here to be sworn in, I asked how much time will I get to speak and they said none," Pelosi said.[1]

She protested to Wright, and he lifted the gag just a little bit, probably because, as the daughter of a former House member and Democratic Party operative, she was hardly unknown to him.

"Keep it short. Keep it short," she recalled being told.[2]

In her very first speech, Pelosi thanked both Phil and Sala Burton, her mentors, who were responsible for her very presence in the chamber. Then, she proceeded to lay out an agenda reflective of San Francisco's needs and the things she would be fighting for as she began her elective political career.

She promised to continue the liberal tradition of the Burtons. She told the members of Congress that "Sala Burton sent me" and promised to continue the Burtons' "leadership for peace, for environmental protection, for equal rights and now to take the leadership in the crisis of AIDS."[3]

At the time, President Ronald Reagan was in the last years of his second term, and the presidential campaign of 1987–88 was heating up. And the Iran-Contra scandal, which played a small role in her election, was boiling over in the Senate, on the other side of the Capitol from where Pelosi was solemnly taking her oath of office. Lt. Col. Oliver North, who had masterminded the "arms for hostages" deal with Iran and then tried to direct the proceeds to the Nicaraguan Contra rebels, was testifying at about the time of her election to Congress, and the country was reeling from the knowledge that the president might have broken a law prohibiting the transaction.

But she didn't mention all of that in her speech, preferring to concentrate on the key domestic issue that were of paramount importance to her San Francisco district, particularly the AIDS crisis, which was hitting the city, with its large homosexual population, harder than most other places.

"We are very proud of the Fifth Congressional District and its leadership for peace, for environmental protection, for equal rights, for rights of individual freedom and now we must take the leadership of course in the crisis of AIDS," she told the House in her 10-sentence statement.

The authoritative "Almanac of American Politics" noted that Pelosi was the "least senior member of Congress" but added that she "gives every sign of being able and effective and of aptly representing this most American of cities as it undergoes yet another American transformation."

She was given seats on the House Banking, Housing, Finance, and Urban Affairs Committee and the Government Operations Committee. They were not very prestigious panels, but fitting for the member of the House with the least seniority. While some of her supporters in San Francisco voiced concerns that serving on the Banking Committee would only underscore the image of Pelosi as a rich representative with scant experience in everyday finance, she had another view.

She thought that her San Francisco constituents would benefit from her position on the committee because of its emphasis on housing issues.

Following her swearing-in, Pelosi immediately added her name to a number of bills that were important to her as a San Francisco legislator. While adding her name was symbolic, the issues were not. They were the ones that would occupy much of her attention during her first years in Congress.

She signed on as a co-sponsor of measures to ban discrimination against gays, to prohibit oil drilling off the California coast, to increase the minimum wage, and to require a moratorium on nuclear weapons testing.

She was embraced on the floor not only by members of the California delegation but also by members of the Maryland delegation, who saw in her the Baltimore native that she was and immediately proclaimed her an honorary Maryland representative.

"We were very excited when she came to Congress," Steny Hoyer remembered. "All of the Maryland delegation was. We did then and we still do think of Nancy as a Marylander."[4]

Sen. Barbara Mikulski, D-Md., noted that both of them went to the Institute of Notre Dame in Baltimore, though four years apart. "Same school, different prom," Mikulski said.[5]

Throughout the day, Pelosi's husband, Paul, hovered around, proud and satisfied with his role as congressional spouse.

"He encouraged her to run," remembered Naomi Lauter, Pelosi's old neighbor. "And he was completely supportive."[6]

For her first hire as a member of Congress, Pelosi employed what was thought at the time to be the first full-time congressional staffer concentrating exclusively on the AIDS issue.

Steve Morin, a San Francisco psychologist, AIDS researcher, and lobbyist on AIDS issues, began work in mid-June 1987, fulfilling a campaign promise made by Pelosi. It was an acknowledgement of her victory over an openly gay opponent and her desire to show that she, too, would make AIDS her cause, and also an acknowledgement of the growing gay community in San Francisco and of the devastating disease that was hitting her city.[7]

The virus, first reported in California in 1981, was racing through San Francisco in the mid 1980s. By 1983, the infection rate in San Francisco's gay population was increasing 18 percent every year. At that time, the disease was thought to be confined to homosexuals, and there was no cure.

Just as Pelosi was taking office, the first drug known to inhibit the HIV virus that causes AIDS was coming into use. Known as AZT, it slowed the spread of the virus but did not arrest it completely.

People were still dying at an alarming rate and by mid-2000, it was estimated that at least 18,000 San Franciscans had died of AIDS—six times the number of people who had died in the great San Francisco fire 100 years earlier.

Was it any wonder, then, that Pelosi's first months in Congress were largely dedicated to helping AIDS victims and looking for funds for medical research into the disease?

For example, at a committee hearing later that first year of her first term, Pelosi gave Reagan administration officials grief about their refusal to widely distribute an AIDS education booklet. Among other things, the booklet gave precise advice on how to prevent the disease, including a recommendation that high-risk groups use a condom.

Pelosi said it took her office months to get hold of 300,000 of the booklets, with one official telling her she couldn't have them because they weren't folded yet. Pelosi offered to do the folding herself.[8]

She gave great publicity to the AIDS epidemic by speaking out. She hoped that by publicizing the crisis, she could help bring it out from the shadows and win funding for research into treatments.

One of Pelosi's first legislative victories was the creation of the Housing Opportunities for People with AIDS program.

Because she represented San Francisco, Pelosi immediately came to the forefront of the AIDS issue, despite being new in Congress. When the Reagan administration refused to distribute literature to every household in the nation outlining the disease and what steps could be taken to prevent transmission from person to person, Pelosi was extremely critical. She also took issue with the Reagan administration's stand on proposed legislation that would have outlawed discrimination against people with AIDS.

The Secretary of Health and Human Services at the time, Otis Bowen, testified at a congressional hearing that such legislation should be handled by the states, not by the federal government, to figure out what works best.

That brought scoffs from Pelosi, who said that Bowen's words showed that he "does not understand the AIDS virus and how it is transmitted."

"It's an old saying that people can die of ignorance," she said. "Theirs and his [Bowen's]."[9]

Pelosi also was getting a crash course in the banking industry, because she got a seat on the House Banking Committee and was immediately thrown into many issues involving the financial community.

She didn't pretend to be an expert, but she threw herself into the issues with the same energy she had always brought to her work.

For example, Congress was considering whether to cap interest rates on credit cards, which on the surface seemed like a good thing for consumers and appealed to Pelosi. But banks argued that if they were limited on how much they could charge, they would restrict credit cards to only certain customers, hurting many ordinary consumers.

In the end, Pelosi's dilemma turned out to reflect the overall Congress's dilemma as well. The cap didn't pass, but Congress enacted a law requiring credit card companies to fully disclose all the terms of their interest rates.

Other than banking, she was concentrating in her first months on the job on issues that directly affected San Francisco.

She led the effort to get the San Francisco Mint—the place where they make coins—declared an actual mint. Despite its name, the mint was in fact an "Assay Office" and was subject to cuts in federal funding. True mint status would protect about 700 jobs and make the building a historical landmark.

In April 1988, she got a big thrill when John Burton, her mentor and friend, won back his old seat in the California Assembly. Burton had been through many difficulties, including bouts with drug and alcohol use, and had left his seat in Congress several years before due to his erratic behavior. But he sought treatment for his addictions and had come through the ordeal. All the while, Pelosi never abandoned him, and he was invaluable to her in her campaign.

He said later that he had such fun working in Pelosi's campaign that he decided to jump back into the political pond when San Francisco Mayor Art Agnos left his assembly seat to run for mayor. Agnos was inaugurated in January 1988 but declined to endorse a potential successor. Burton fought off charges that he was a "machine" politician who had assembled an "old-boy" network. He put together a coalition of ethnic minorities, labor, environmentalists, and senior citizens to win. It had to have made Pelosi very happy.[10]

But all was not happiness for Pelosi in her first term. Just as she was getting started in her congressional career, her father, who had become her political role model when she decided to move from being a behind-the-scenes operative to being a candidate, died of heart failure in August 1987. Just two short months before, the House had given him two standing ovations when Pelosi referred to him in her opening speech. Now, it was her chance to eulogize him. She said that her father was a man motivated by "love and commitment to people."

"In the vitality of the city that he loved and the commitment to the people which he shared and the laughter of his grandchildren, Tommy D'Alesandro lives," she said.[11]

In a way, it was as if she were talking about her life to come in the next 20 years.

NOTES

1. Edward Epstein, "Pelosi Marks Milestone, Having Risen from Quiet Obscurity to Become House's Leading Voice," *San Francisco Chronicle*, June 10, 2007, p. A17.

2. Ibid.

3. Larry Liebert, "Pelosi Takes Office/House Embraces Its Newest Member," *San Francisco Chronicle*, June 10, 1987, p. 11.

4. Steny Hoyer, interview with author, Washington, D.C., October 24, 2007.

5. Ibid.

6. Naomi Lauter, interview with author, San Francisco, November 5, 2007.

7. Dawn Garcia, "Pelosi Hires Staffer to Work on AIDS," *San Francisco Chronicle*, June 20, 1987, p. 5.

8. Susan Sward, "Guilty of Murder/Administration Hit on AIDS Education," *San Francisco Chronicle*, November 24, 1987, p. 7.

9. Coimbra M. Sirica, "Guilty of Murder," *San Francisco Chronicle*, September 22, 1987, p. A7.

10. Jerry Roberts and Mark Z. Barabak, "John Burton Recaptures His Old Assembly Seat," *San Francisco Chronicle*, April 13, 1988, p. A1.

11. "D'Alesandro Funeral Mass—Pelosi Gives Eulogy for Father," *Baltimore Sun*, August 27, 1987, p. 44.

Chapter 6

EARTHQUAKE!

Nancy Pelosi had been in office only about two years when her hometown suffered a major earthquake, the Loma Prieta quake that hit on October 17, 1989, at just after 5 P.M. It lasted about 15 seconds and measured 6.9 on the scale that judges severity of earthquakes. A 6.9 quake is a big one! The Loma Prieta earthquake killed 63 people throughout northern California—most in San Francisco—and left more than 12,000 homeless.

It occurred during warm-ups for the third game of the 1989 World Series, with two San Francisco Bay area teams—the Oakland Athletics and the San Francisco Giants—competing. Many Americans' television sets were tuned to the pre-game festivities when the entire stadium began to shake.

Much of the rest of the city was shaking, too.

Pelosi was in Washington, having dinner with a group of legislators who were part of a long-standing Tuesday night tradition. The group was hosted by former Rep. Tom Downey of Long Island, N.Y., who had a row house in the Capitol Hill section of Washington, not far from the Capitol itself. Other California legislators, including Rep. Barbara Boxer, a fellow Democrat from nearby Marin County, were at the dinner, as well.

The group was sitting down to wine and pasta as news of the earthquake came on the television.

"Nancy and Barbara were naturally worried because their husbands and family members were all at the [World Series] game," Downey recalled. "I had a big satellite dish at the time, and we were able to get the San Francisco news feeds to see what was going on."[1]

It was a mess, but Pelosi swung into action. First, she got on a plane in Washington and headed home to San Francisco. Once there, she began assessing the damage, reporting back to her Washington colleagues that things were pretty bad out there but that there was work to be done and no one should wait.

In a statement for the Congressional Record, Pelosi made sure her colleagues knew that it was the second deadliest earthquake in U.S. history (the first one was in San Francisco, too, in 1906), a precursor of relief requests that would be coming soon.

"President Bush has declared the San Francisco Bay area a disaster area," she said. "I look forward to the support of my colleagues in my efforts to obtain Federal support to restore San Francisco and other affected areas."[2]

Several days later, Pelosi and other California representatives, having gotten a better handle on the damage, began their crusade for rebuilding.

The quake caused about $6 billion in initial property damage. Private donations poured into the city, and President George H. W. Bush signed a $3.45 billion earthquake relief package for San Francisco and other parts of California that were affected. It would be only the beginning.

In particular, Pelosi pointed out the extensive damage to the Marina district of San Francisco, a part of the city that ironically was built on landfill created after the 1906 San Francisco earthquake. She noted, for House members who might not have been familiar with the Marina district of her city, just how important it was, particularly to baseball fans, since that was the home of the Yankees' 1930s and 1940s great Joe DiMaggio, a native of San Francisco.

DiMaggio, she noted, was at the ballpark waiting for the World Series to begin when the quake hit. DiMaggio, like so many in the park, rushed home to the Marina district to see what had happened to his house. And he, like everyone else, was prohibited from entering the home by authorities who were trying to determine if it was structurally safe. By telling this story, Pelosi brought the earthquake home to her colleagues and the rest of the world, who, even having seen the pictures of the awful destruction—including a collapsed freeway—on television, needed to know more.

And there was more to the Marina district for Pelosi, because that's how her husband, Paul, described himself when they first met. "My husband, Paul, is a Marina kid," she said, remembering that's how he introduced himself to her. "I asked him what part of California he was from," she recalled. "He responded that he was from the Marina district of San Francisco, as if we would know what that meant."

The Marina also was home to many Italian-Americans, giving Pelosi even more impetus to try to help victims there.[3]

Michael Yaki, who was Pelosi's district director at the time, said that Pelosi was quick to figure out that the congresswoman's office had to be intimately involved in the relief efforts, not only in Washington looking for federal money, but also in San Francisco, where her office took a hands-on approach.

For example, Yaki said, the Federal Emergency Management Agency initially wanted to local its emergency services office on the complete other side of town from the Marina district, where most of the damage was. That location was particularly hard for Marina residents to reach because there are few roads in San Francisco that lead from the area near the Bay across town.

Yaki said Pelosi and her staff recognized this problem instantly and insisted that the office be located at the Presidio Army Base, adjacent to the Marina district.[4]

Communication from Washington emergency agencies like FEMA also proved difficult, so Pelosi's office starting putting out its own flyers on how to apply for federal disaster loans and other assistance and served as a clearinghouse for distraught earthquake victims who had lost so much.

Pelosi had to fight the battles one by one to restore her city. For example, the federal agencies didn't want to give disaster money to restore the historic Geary Theater, home to the famous American Theater Company, which had been damaged in the quake, saying that the law prevented an expenditure of federal funds for theaters. Pelosi had her staff research the law, and it turned out that, in fact, theaters could get money. The theater was restored. John Sullivan, managing director of the theater from 1986 to 1993, generously gave Pelosi and her staff most of the credit.

"I stayed through the completion of getting the federal funding, did a lot of work with Nancy Pelosi and her staff on the FEMA grant. At the time the largest grant that FEMA had given to a not-for-profit was $5,000," Sullivan recalled for a celebration of the theater's fortieth anniversary, in 2006. "We got $10 million and it was a real push."[5]

Once the theater had been restored to its original beauty and was again open to productions, the theater managers decided to dedicate a stained glass window to Pelosi, to honor her work in the restoration.

Another big fight that came out of the restoration of San Francisco after the earthquake was what to do about San Francisco's City Hall, an iconic building that had been badly damaged in the quake. FEMA's initial offer to repair the damage was $2 million, Yaki recalled, "which amounted to a spackle job." But to bring the building up to current codes, required by federal law, would have required $120 million, and Pelosi was "relentless" in her pursuit of the money. The City of San Francisco chipped in $100 million, as well, and City Hall was restored. By the time the project was done, underground rollers were installed under the foundation of the building so that if there was ever another earthquake the strength of the Loma Prieta trembler, the building would "roll" slightly, rather than cracking apart.

"It was her first real test under fire and she passed with flying colors," Yaki said.[6]

There would be more tests, as the funding effort to repair the earthquake damage and get ready for the next inevitable major quake along the San Andreas Fault dragged on for years.

In September 1992, three years after the quake, San Francisco officials were still fighting for money.

City officials insisted that 1.7 miles of underground cast-iron water pipe, which had been broken in 60 places by the quake, be completely replaced with a new plastic pipe at a cost of $937,000. But FEMA initially wanted to pay only $172,000.

Pelosi and city officials had to point out to the agency that if the old pipe was patched up, it would probably break again. Eventually, they got the extra money.

And the city had to sue the federal government over paying for the cost of repairing single-room-occupancy hotels, which the city had leased to house the homeless. FEMA argued that the hotels were neither public nor nonprofit structures eligible for federal money. But the city eventually won.

"Our experience is that FEMA and OMB [the Office of Management and Budget] used the law as an obstacle," said Pelosi. "The tragedy of all this is that it can be dragged on for a long time, a very long time."[7]

And even as late as 2002—fully five years later—Pelosi was still successfully fighting for funds. In July of that year, she announced that she and several other representatives from the area had succeeded in directing $6.5 million in new "seismic retrofit" funding to upgrade the Golden Gate Bridge, San Francisco's symbolic structure.

Pelosi noted in announcing the grant that the bridge had been stressed almost to its breaking point by the Loma Prieta earthquake and that any more stress on the bridge, without the upgrades, could be catastrophic.

"The Golden Gate Bridge is an essential corridor for commerce and recreation in the Bay Area as well as a beloved national symbol," she said. "These funds will help ensure that in case of an earthquake many lives will be saved, and the bridge will survive."[8]

Part of the reason that Pelosi was able to get so much funding for things in her district was that at the end of 1990, she was appointed to the powerful House Appropriations Committee. That committee is so powerful on Capitol Hill that the chairmen of its 13 subcommittees are called "cardinals," and legislators make a figurative attempt to kiss their rings if they want things for their hometowns.

Pelosi, as a member of the panel, was able to trade favors with others and get things that she wanted. It was very much the kind of insiders' game that she was used to as a party operative, and it relied on people making promises and keeping their word—two other things at which Pelosi excelled and two things that were critical to congressional success.

She had really "arrived," in the way people in Congress speak, by getting a seat on appropriations. Her father would have been pleased as well, since that committee is where he once served.

"It's important to my district and to the state of California," Pelosi said at the time of her new assignment. "From the standpoint of health, housing, transportation, it's important for us to be part of the decision-making. In times of tight fiscal policy, it's even more important to be at the table."[9]

She had sought a place on the committee earlier in 1990 but was edged out by another woman member of Congress, Marcy Kaptur of Ohio, who had more seniority. But, later, House Speaker Thomas P. "Tip" O'Neill, who had always favored Pelosi, announced that he would be expanding membership on the panel, all but guaranteeing Pelosi the seat that she eventually got.

She knew right away the importance of the panel in that she could start asking other people for things because they would also be asking her for favors.

Over the years, Pelosi was able to obtain millions of government dollars for projects in San Francisco, including some that were controversial. She took some heat later in her career, for example, for tacking on a $1 million appropriation for a think tank in San Francisco started by her long-time mentor, former Lt. Gov. Leo McCarthy. It was typical of the kind of item that appropriations committee members are famous for, but it did bring her a little heat.

Nonetheless, the $1 million appropriation for the Center for Public Service and the Common Good at the University of San Francisco was approved. It was among thousands of items buried in the 3,000-page, $397.4 billion omnibus appropriations bill that Congress passed in 2003.

Pelosi made no apologies for it. Her standard justification was that projects like the think tank are going to get federal money, anyway, and the money might as well go to her hometown.

She worked the system perfectly to gain some of that money.

But, early in her career, she found out there was one high-profile place in her district that she couldn't save. She had to get creative.

NOTES

1. Zachary Coile, "Pelosi Seeks Input from Diverse Array of Confidants," *San Francisco Chronicle*, December 19, 2006, p. A1.

2. Congressional Record, October 18, 1989.

3. Congressional Record, October 23, 1989.

4. Michael Yaki, interview with author, San Francisco, November 10, 2007.

5. Robert Hurwitt, "The Long Run Act; A 'Madman's' Vision," *San Francisco Chronicle*, October 8, 2006, p. 1.

6. Michael Yaki, interview with author, San Francisco, November 10, 2007.

7. Edmund Andrews, "After the Storm: Victims of 1989 Earthquake and Hurricane Are Still Fighting for Federal Aid," *New York Times*, September 7, 1992, p. A1.

8. Office of Rep. Nancy Pelosi, press release, July 9, 2002.

9. Larry Liebert, "Nancy Pelosi Has Finally Arrived on Capitol Hill," *San Francisco Chronicle*, December 13, 1990, p. A29.

Chapter 7

THE PRESIDIO

The Presidio in San Francisco was among the most beautiful and historic U.S. military bases in the world. With a stunning view of San Francisco Bay and the Golden Gate Bridge, the Presidio (which means "garrison" in Spanish) was home to some of the most important military officials and the scene of some of the most glittery military parties over more than 100 years, from 1846 to 1994.

In 1861, the outbreak of the Civil War meant many improvements to the Presidio, and a fort was built there, designed to hold 126 cannon, at the mouth of the bay. There were no battles of the Civil War at the Presidio, but it continued to be a prestigious base. By the 1890s, it had become a major military installation.

During the 1898 Spanish-American War, troops—including four African American "Buffalo Soldier" regiments—massed at the Presidio before heading for the Philippines.

The Presidio also played an important role in the 1906 San Francisco earthquake, when the Army provided food, shelter, and clothing for victims. By 1941, the base was modernized, and, after the Japanese attack on Pearl Harbor, when many people thought an attack on the West Coast of the United States was next, the Presidio dug in for a possible defensive action. In the 1950s, the Presidio was headquarters for a missile defense system, as well as the headquarters for the famed Sixth U.S. Army division.[1]

But by the early 1990s, the Presidio, like many military bases around the country, had outlived its usefulness. A bipartisan commission was formed by Congress to recommend that many military bases be closed or consolidated. The commission was formed because Congress didn't have the political will to tackle such a controversial endeavor. Members of Congress knew that shutting down bases would mean the loss of a lot of jobs in their areas, and they didn't want to be responsible for that.

The commission issued its recommendations, and the rule was that Congress had to "take it or leave it," meaning that all of the bases had to be closed or none of them would be. As much as Congress wanted to save money, the decisions to close the bases were very controversial.

Nowhere was that controversy more fierce than over the Presidio. There were many factors at work. First, the Presidio was the 200-year-old gleaming jewel of the American armed forces, and many prestigious military leaders had been attached to it. In addition, it had such a storied history. And, it was the fifth largest employer in San Francisco—and that meant more than 5,000 people would lose their jobs if it were closed.

But San Francisco had changed dramatically over the years. The military was no longer a high priority for many of the citizens of the city. San Francisco was home to many people who were opposed to war in any form, and that made it difficult for them to turn around and insist that the base be kept open.

That didn't mean that Pelosi and her colleague then Rep. Barbara Boxer, from nearby Marin County, Calif., didn't want to try. For Pelosi, there was a sentimental reason, as well—her mentors, Phil and Sala Burton, were buried on that scenic site.

The first thing they tried was a study. In February 1989, the two released a report that said that it would cost $26 million a year to close down the Presidio, countering an initial report that said that shutting the base down would save $74 million annually.

With a great deal of fanfare, the two announced the results of the study in San Francisco, countering arguments by taxpayer groups that closing the base would save many millions of dollars.

Pelosi and Boxer were setting out their arguments in advance of congressional hearings on the base closings, and in advance of yet another study that was going to be critical to the efforts to close the bases. The deck was stacked against them.

Buffeted by pleas like Pelosi's from many areas of the country, eventually the Congress decided to abide by the commission's recommendations and close 86 military bases across the country, including the Presidio.

Pelosi signaled that she and Boxer might try to block actual funds from being used to do the shutdown, but congressional leaders at the time were on to her plan and warned sternly against it.

"We're interested in making sure there is no fooling around with this list, and we're going to be watching all legislation from now on to make sure there is no end run," counseled Representative Les Aspin, D-Wis., chairman of the House Armed Services Committee.[2]

But Rep. John Murtha, D-Pa., one of the "cardinals" on the House Appropriations Committee, seemed sympathetic. Murtha headed the sub-committee that dealt in defense spending, and he was key to Boxer and Pelosi's effort.

"We were concerned they were just being parochial," Murtha said at the time. "But if these figures are correct, then it does not make sense to close the base."[3]

Murtha's sympathy to Pelosi's cause was the beginning of a relationship that would endure for years, up to and including her Speakership. She and Murtha would cross paths on many issues—fundraising and the war in Iraq included. They also served together on the Appropriations Commit-tee after Pelosi got her appointment there. But their relationship began with the Presidio.

Despite congressional desires to keep the base-closings package to-gether, Murtha himself offered an amendment in his own committee that would have prohibited funds from being used to shut down the Presidio, unless a study found that the shutdown would start saving the govern-ment money in six years, minus the costs of shutdown.

It was a victory for Pelosi, but, in the end, her efforts and those of Boxer were not enough to stop the shutdown. Eventually, the Presidio was closed as a military base.

But Pelosi had another trick in her pocket. Her mentor and predecessor in the congressional seat, Phil Burton, in a prescient move that showcased his political and practical savvy, had managed to pass a law back in the 1970s that called for the Presidio to be turned over to the National Park Service if it ever was closed as a military base.

While other cities and states around that nation bickered over what to do with shuttered military bases—some turned them into housing tracts or industrial parks or commercial airports—there was a plan for the Pre-sidio. That plan traded on the Presidio's unique character and placement on the California coastline.

But the Park Service was in uncharted territory when it came to the Presidio. For one thing, Park Service officials estimated it would cost more money to take over the installation and run it than it cost to take care of any other park in the system, including Yosemite. Second, the Presidio, unlike any other national park, had lots of roads and buildings included in it that were decidedly un-park-like.

Encompassing 1,480 acres, the facility had more than 1,000 homes and apartments, two hospitals, two chapels, a bowling alley, and a golf course. In a more park-like feature, it was the home of more than a dozen rare or endangered plants, including the raven manzanita, a shrub with small, white flowers found only on the Presidio grounds.

The Park Service tried to figure out how to best administer the Presidio. The service got some money from Congress to try to take over the facility, but after several years it became apparent that it was going to be far too expensive to maintain such a diverse and different facility.

That's when Pelosi came up with a unique idea—the Presidio Trust.

The plan Pelosi created put together a public-private trust to provide money for the centuries-old military base. In 1994, the bill passed the House but died in the Senate. But, by 1996, the Senate had changed. For one thing, Boxer was now a senator, and with her partner from California, Sen. Dianne Feinstein, also a Democrat, they managed to get the bill passed, and it was signed by President Bill Clinton.

But the plan had a catch—the Presidio had to be self-supporting by 2013.

By the mid-2000s, Pelosi was getting some heat because some of the valuable land and buildings were sold to private companies run by her supporters or friends, but no one could prove that there was anything amiss in the transactions. Much of the beautiful Presidio was destined to be open to the public for generations.

"Today's victory is a victory for our community and for everyone who has yet to walk the Presidio's historic grounds, to marvel at its diverse past and to find solace in its incomparable beauty," Pelosi said when the bill passed Congress.[4]

NOTES

1. From National Park Service Web site, www.nps.gov, "The Presidio of San Francisco, U.S. Military Period, 1846–1994."

2. Larry Liebert, "House Votes to Close Presidio, Other Bases/Pelosi, Boxer Told Not to Try 'End Run,'" *San Francisco Chronicle,* April 19, 1989, p. A1.

3. Dawn Garcia, "New Study Challenges Closing of the Presidio," *San Francisco Chronicle,* February 16, 1989, p. A1.

4. Press Release, Congresswoman Nancy Pelosi, September 28, 1996.

Chapter 8

TIANANMEN SQUARE

"Tiananmen Square" will always conjure up images of a lone Chinese student standing in front of a line of Chinese Army tanks, forcing the tanks to move side to side to avoid running him down. That simple act of non-violent protest came to symbolize the uprising by Chinese students and the bloody crackdown by the Chinese government in June 1989.

Thousands of Chinese civilians had flocked to Tiananmen Square in Beijing over a period of weeks, calling on the Chinese government to institute some democratic reforms to their totalitarian government. While democracy movements had taken hold in some Communist countries at that time, particularly in Eastern Europe, the Chinese leaders were determined that there would be no similar movement in China.

The government tried for seven weeks to get the students to leave the square, but, instead, the reverse happened. More people joined them every day, not just students but doctors, teachers, and other ordinary folk, as well. Finally, the government of the People's Republic of China could not stand it any longer, and it cracked down with a military action. The tanks rumbled into the square. Guns were fired, some said indiscriminately. Estimates vary, but between several hundred and several thousand civilians were shot dead by the Chinese Army during that time, as the soldiers moved in, firing on the unarmed protestors. About 20,000 were injured, and several thousand were taken political prisoner.

Live television showed victims being rushed to hospitals on rickshaws, bicycles, and park benches, carried by terrified civilians.

Pelosi, who had been in the House a little more than a year at the time of the demonstration, found herself in the thick of it because of the large number of Chinese Americans in San Francisco. Because she was well known in the Chinese American community, native Chinese students who were studying in the United States also sought her out.

The Chinese students were terrified to return to China following the Tiananmen crackdown because they feared for their safety, their liberty, and even their lives. Because there was little Internet traffic at that time, Chinese students in America had aided their friends in Beijing during the uprising with information from the outside world, which they were unable to get in China. They had telephones and, especially, facsimile (or fax) machines, on which they transferred critical information. The Chinese students in the United States also served as communication aids within the movement, putting various leaders in touch with one another. But because of their actions, they were afraid the Chinese government would come after them, too, if they returned home.

They descended on Pelosi's office, begging her to find a way that they could stay in the United States once their two-year student visas expired. Pelosi swung into action.

The first thing that happened was that then President George H. W. Bush stopped China from ordering the forcible return of the students to China. He also secretly sent a number of his aides to China to see if there was a way to get the Chinese to let some prisoners out of jail and ease re-strictions. As the president saw it, China could become an important ally on trade, but first it had to get its human rights house in order.

Since no one knew of the mission, no one knew that it had failed. What was obvious was that the Chinese government was determined to crack down on the protesters and on the infant democracy movement in China.

Meanwhile, the American people continued to be outraged at what they had seen on their television of the violence and brutality at Tianan-men Square. A Gallup poll showed that the number of Americans who held a favorable attitude toward China fell from 72 percent in a 1989 poll to about 39 percent after the demonstrations.[1]

On the heels of the Tiananmen Square massacre and prodded by the Chinese American community, Pelosi sponsored a bill to let the Chinese students who were studying in the United States stay longer than their two-year visas allowed. Her measure would have allowed the students to seek permanent residency in the United States without returning home first.

Many of the Chinese students said that their lives would be in danger if they were to return home. Pelosi, sensitive to their plight, decided to take action. It was the first time that she had been thrust into the national limelight as a member of Congress. With only a couple of years' worth of experience, she was suddenly being asked to be a spokesman on China, Tiananmen Square, and human rights.

"What happened was that there was a vacuum in that part of American foreign policy that had always been a part of American foreign policy—the idea of America as a moral leader," said Michael Yaki.[2]

She also started criticizing President Bush. And, instead of ignoring this congresswoman, Bush rose to the bait, and she became the voice of democratic values against China's economic ties to the United States.

She made appearances at rallies and press conferences and on television to champion her bill and stand for democracy.

"All of a sudden, every TV camera, every article, is noticing this one-and-one-half-term congresswoman from San Francisco," Yaki remembered.[3]

On August 1, 1989, the House of Representatives passed the Pelosi bill nearly unanimously on a voice vote. Only two representatives spoke against it.

Pelosi said it would protect 40,000 Chinese students in the United States.

"We have seen the brutality that the Chinese government is capable of inflicting on its own nationals," said Pelosi in a speech on the House floor.[4]

The Senate approved the bill as well, on a voice vote, and all seemed well. But President Bush, citing presidential prerogative and economic considerations such as trade with China, vetoed the bill.

By this time, Pelosi had many, many allies and was continuing to make a name for herself as a champion of human rights. Interestingly, some of her allies were very conservative members of Congress, such as the notoriously conservative Sen. Jesse Helms, a Republican of North Carolina, who were opposed to the Communist regime in China in general. She also had more natural allies, given her liberal outlook, among the liberal members of the House and Senate.

One of those more liberal members was an old friend—Senate Majority Leader George Mitchell, D-Maine, whom she helped into his position by working with him to elect a Democratic majority in the Senate. Mitchell traveled to San Francisco after the congressional vote and the threatened veto and gave a speech to the prestigious Commonwealth Club, where he took Bush to task both for the secret mission to China and for opposing Pelosi's legislation.

At the time, Mitchell predicted success in overriding the president's veto, telling reporters that "I believe the merits of the issue are so clear and the president's decision so unwise."[5]

But Mitchell and Pelosi had underestimated Bush's clout with Republicans, particularly those in the Senate. At the time, Bush was very popular, and he couched his arguments in a way that put Senate Republicans in a tough spot. He said they shouldn't undermine his power in dealing with the Chinese government. He also said that if they overrode the veto and cut his power in foreign affairs, it would have an adverse impact on his ability to get other things done. He also promised to continue to issue executive orders to protect the Chinese students.

He wrote individual letters to members of the Senate, promising he wouldn't deport a single Chinese student if they would just sustain his veto of Pelosi's bill. It was an enormous amount of attention to be paid to the relatively inexperienced congresswoman, and it put her on the map.

"It was like you riding a bicycle and all of a sudden it sprouted rockets," Yaki said. "It was the rocket-fueled booster that pushed her into the spotlight."[6]

In addition, Bush got former presidents like Richard Nixon, who had made the first overtures to China back in the 1970s, to call senators and say that the president must be able to be flexible in dealing with China. It worked, and the Senate fell four votes shy of overriding the veto. But Bush, true to his word, did issue orders prohibiting the Chinese students from being sent back against their will.

Pelosi said the fight had been worth it, if for no other reason than it highlighted the plight of the Chinese in the aftermath of Tiananmen Square. It also solidified her as a champion of human rights, and the debate put her on center stage. She said the debate had been important, too, because it forced Bush to protect the students, even though her bill didn't pass.

But Pelosi was criticized, as well. Some people said that she had used the human rights issue as a self-promotion tool. She denied it, saying that she had always been a champion of human rights, going back to the days when she was rolling her kids around in strollers and working for Democratic causes.

"I raised my children outside of consulates and embassies, where we could protest repression in any country around the world," she said at the time. "In San Francisco, we were regulars outside the Soviet Consulate. We picketed the civic dinner in honor of Ferdinand Marcos when he came to City Hall."

Although her direct influence on China issues remained slight, Pelosi said she wouldn't quit.

"They can say what they want," Pelosi said. "Some people say to me, 'Do you ever get tired?' I say the case is more conclusive than ever. The longer the repression continues, the larger the trade deficits and the other violations continue, the more proliferation that China engages in, the stronger the case that U.S. policy is not a success."[7]

Pelosi continued to highlight human rights violations in China. In 1991, she traveled to Beijing and went to see Tiananmen Square for herself. Along with about 20 other members of Congress, Pelosi unwound a banner that read "To those who died for democracy in China."

She and the others were immediately surrounded by police and by government officials who were posing as tourists.

"I started running," Pelosi said right after the incident, "and my colleagues, some of them, got a little roughed up. The press got treated worse because they had cameras, and they were detained."

The Chinese Foreign Ministry denounced the incident as a "premeditated farce." But the delegation wasn't arrested and wasn't jailed. Pelosi had made her point.

She often referred to that event to illustrate the China wasn't above harassing members of the U.S. Congress.[8]

CHINA TRADE

After the bruising fight over immigration status for Chinese students, it became clear that the Bush administration's motivating factor in dealing with the Chinese was clearly economic. A year after the student visa debate, an issue came up with regard to trade with China.

In international trade, a nation that imposes low tariffs or taxes on goods traded with another nation is said to have "most favored nation" trading status with that second nation. Almost all countries in the world want to have favorable trading status with the United States, because the it has the largest consumer market in the world, and, in order to sell cheap goods in the United States, low tariffs are a must.

Presidents are allowed to negotiate trade treaties with other countries, and Congress can't do much about it until the treaties are signed. But after that, if Congress wants to disapprove of a trade pact, it can.

In 1991, Pelosi took the lead on a move to condition China's favorable trade treatment on improvements in its record on human rights issue. Her bill on the issue passed both houses of Congress but was vetoed by President George H. W. Bush. The House voted to override the veto 257–61, but the Senate again upheld the president, and the bill died.

By 1992, there was a new president, Bill Clinton, and he was a Democrat who had campaigned on pressing for better human rights in China and the release of political prisoners. But Clinton, too, decided to renew

China's trade status, and again Pelosi found herself opposing a president—but this time it was one of her own party.

Undaunted, she called Clinton's 1995 round of trade talks with China a "failure."[9]

She continued to push for human rights improvements in China, sometimes working with Senate Majority Leader Mitchell, sometimes with unlikely conservative Republican allies, sometimes with Democrats. She had high hopes that Clinton would press as hard as she had for human rights in China. But, in the end, economics again triumphed, as trade with China continued. However, Clinton and his administration did continue to push China to ease up on dissidents and to join with other nations around the world for better relations and more freedom.

In 1997, her fight continued, even though it put her at odds with California's Democratic senator, Dianne Feinstein. Feinstein's husband, a businessman, had many business dealings with China, and she appeared to believe that the way to get China to change its ways was through economic interaction. But Pelosi took the opposite tack, believing that depriving China of trade benefits would awaken the Chinese government to the idea that it had to change its dismal human rights record. While Feinstein attended a state dinner at the White House that year honoring the Chinese president, Jiang Zemin, Pelosi refused. Instead, she went to a human rights rally in Lafayette Park, across the street.[10]

That protest was part of her continuing crusade for human rights in China. She drew some satisfaction from some mild improvements there. Year after year, she saw China's trade status renewed despite human rights violations but continued to fight.

"The Clinton Administration and the Chinese regime should take no comfort from the outcome of this vote," she said at a press conference after one trade law was renewed in the 1990s. "Regardless of the quantitative outcome, our vote is qualitatively stronger because we've increased the awareness in Congress and among the American people of the key issues like trade, proliferation, and religious and human rights."

NOTES

1. David Skidmore and William Gates, "After Tiananmen: The Struggle over U.S. Policy toward China in the Bush Administration," *Presidential Studies Quarterly*, vol. 27 (1997).

2. Michael Yaki, interview with author, San Francisco, November 3, 2007.

3. Ibid.

4. Larry Liebert, "Visa Extensions/House OKs Help for China Students," *San Francisco Chronicle*, August 1, 1989, p. A9.

5. Mark Z. Barabak, "Speech to S.F. Group/Sen. Mitchell Rips Bush on China Mission," *San Francisco Chronicle*, December 14, 1989, p. A20.

6. Michael Yaki, interview with author, San Francisco, November 3, 2007.

7. Robert Salladay, "Pelosi on China: A Voice in the Global Wilderness?" *San Francisco Examiner*, June 28, 1998, p. A1.

8. Ibid.

9. Michael Barone and Grant Ujifusa, "The Almanac of American Politics, 1990," National Journal Group, Inc., Washington, D.C., pp. 113–116.

10. Elaine Sciolino, "A Chinese Visitor Comes between Longtime California Allies," *New York Times*, October 30, 1997. Available at: http://query.nytimes.com/gst.

Chapter 9

AIDS

When Pelosi came to Congress, in 1987, with AIDS and HIV at the top of her agenda, she probably had no idea that 20 years later, she would still be dealing with the issue. It was not all-consuming, because she had branched out into many areas, but it was always there.

In 1987, hopes were high that a cure or a vaccine for the devastating disease would be found. Some drugs had been manufactured that slowed the progress of the illness—people with AIDS were living longer—but two decades later, there was no permanent prevention or cure.

Pelosi gave many speeches about those who were close to her who had died. None was more poignant than the tribute she paid to Bob Hattoy, a leading environmentalist from California, who publicly acknowledged his disease at the Democratic convention in 1992 and then went to work for President Bill Clinton in the White House.

Hattoy's roots, however, were in California, and that's where Pelosi came to know him. The two spoke together in 1996 at the dedication of the National AIDS Memorial Grove in San Francisco's Golden Gate Park. Hattoy said that as a gay man with AIDS, nothing could be more important to him than designating quiet, peaceful memorials where people could go to heal and renew their energy for the fight for access to life-prolonging drugs.

Pelosi, who co-authored the bill giving the 15-acre wooded area the same protected status as other national monuments like Mt. Rushmore, spoke with some optimism, reflecting her indefatigable spirit. "We have made AIDS a nonpartisan issue," she said. "Our challenge is to make sure there are drugs for everyone."[1]

But drugs and care could not save Hattoy, and in 2007, he became one of the approximately 20,000 people to date in the San Francisco Bay area to die of AIDS.

"I am proud to have called Bob my dear friend for many years," Pelosi said at his memorial service. "Since we lost Bob, many of us here have been sharing years of stories, anecdotes, and witticisms. Bob's insights were often off-color, yet always on the mark. Bob loved people and had a gift for using humor to face the most serious of life's challenges with a light heart."

She told how she had talked to Hattoy just 100 days earlier and he was "hopeful" about her and about the Democrats in Congress. "We reflected briefly—and humorously—on some of the political events of the past 20 years, and Bob expressed great hopes for the new Congress, and for the challenges we were preparing to address. Although he lived with AIDS for more than 15 years, AIDS took Bob from us too soon."[2]

It was deaths like Hattoy's that kept Pelosi in the fight over the course of her career in Congress for more money, more drugs, more research, and more assistance for those with AIDS.

On June 1, 2006, the twentieth anniversary of the first official AIDS diagnosis, Pelosi spoke about the AIDS quilt, a tapestry made by friends and loved ones to honor those who have died of AIDS. Each patch in the quilt represents a different person.

Pelosi recalled how the AIDS activist Cleve Jones came to her shortly after her election with the quilt idea.

" 'Nobody sews,' I told him. I have four daughters, I was taught to sew in Catholic School, but nobody sews anymore. Little did I know. And he says, 'Oh yes, they will sew. Each panel will be a tribute.'

"Two years later, in 1989, we were in front of the National Park Service saying, 'I don't care how many tons this quilt weighs. We want it on the Mall.' They were saying we were going to kill the grass, and we promised we would lift it up every 30 minutes.

"Imagine in that two years...tons of patches for this quilt. Cleve was working on it during the week, and even I made a quilt for the flower girl in my wedding who died of AIDS," Pelosi said.[3]

That quilt section, dedicated to Susan Piracci Roggio, is a simple patchwork with browns, grays, and a splash of red, with Roggio's name written diagonally across the rectangular cloth in green letters styled with small flares at the bottom of the "I's."[4]

Pelosi had been touched both personally and professionally by this devastating disease.

Pelosi's involvement in the AIDS began with her first speech in Congress and continued throughout her career. Her constituency in San Francisco had so many gay people in it that the issue was impossible to ignore. The longer she stayed in Congress, the more deeply she got into the AIDS issue.

She hired Steve Morin, a medical doctor and researcher who was involved in the issue, to spearhead her efforts. Morin started when Pelosi came to office in 1987 and stayed for a decade. When he left, she hired other people to concentrate on AIDS.

She got some grief initially for citing AIDS in her first speech to Congress. She was asked how she could put that then controversial disease into her maiden speech. She responded that she could not afford not to talk about it—it was consuming her city.

She started out by gathering together people in the San Francisco community who were knowledgeable about AIDS. Either they were living with the disease themselves, or knew someone who was, or were involved through clinics or other gathering places for those battling the disease.

Her first legislative effort involved helping the public health service to develop treatment guidelines for AIDS. The treatments at that time were so experimental that many doctors were just going out on their own and trying various drugs to see what worked best. Pelosi's effort nationalized the treatment guidelines and gave physicians something to turn to other than their own experience when trying to treat patients.

Her second bill established demonstration projects that looked at the psychological and mental health issues that surrounded AIDS, a program that was still running more than 20 years later.

These accomplishments, though relatively small, came at a time when AIDS was considered by some to be a "punishment" for being gay. President Ronald Reagan never even mentioned the disease until late in 1987, even though it had been raging for years with no cure. Even after his friend from his Hollywood days, Rock Hudson, died from AIDS in 1985, Reagan continued his silence. Officials in his administration did very little to even acknowledge the disease, let alone increase funding.

Pelosi was not deterred by any of this. In fact, one of the reasons she went after a seat on the Appropriations Committee was that she understood that if she got there, she could get on the health subcommittee and get more money for AIDS. She did all of that, and by 1990 she had won the coveted seat on Appropriations.

"Appropriations was part of the strategy," said Morin. "She knew exactly where she wanted to be and organized accordingly. That ultimately gave her more standing to influence AIDS policy. That's why she had success so early in her career."[5]

Her first major bill was called the AIDS Health Care Financing Act." It didn't pass the Congress, but it was a precursor to the so-called Ryan White Act, the first major bill to provide federal money for AIDS. Passed in 1990, the Ryan White Act was named after an Indiana hemophiliac teenager who got the virus from a tainted blood transfusion used to treat his hemophilia. White was the perfect "poster boy" for the disease. First of all, he wasn't gay, debunking the myth that AIDS was only a gay person's disease, and second, he was a cute kid from the heartland of the country who evoked universal sympathy.

The Ryan White Act provided as much as $875 million to help state and local governments cope with the AIDS epidemic, the first time the federal government had gotten involved in a major way.

"This legislation is a breakthrough in AIDS treatment," Pelosi said at the time.[6]

The bill initially provided money only to places where the virus was rampant—San Francisco, New York, Los Angeles, and 13 other big cities. But it was a huge step.

With the funding source established, Pelosi continued to work through the late 1990s on getting more money for AIDS treatment and research. She also began a controversial crusade for needle exchange programs. Research into the transmission of the AIDS virus had shown that intravenous drug users often passed the disease along to others by sharing needles. If an infected person injected himself with the needle, then passed it to a friend, the friend was likely to become infected, too.

Pelosi argued that federal money was needed to help cities fund needle exchange programs under which a drug user could bring used needles to a checkpoint and get clean ones in return, without fear of arrest. Pelosi said such a program would slow down transmission of the AIDS virus but would not increase drug use. However, the House of Representatives refused to pass her bill in 1997.

With Republicans now in charge of Congress, funding for many programs was imperiled, and none so much as money for AIDS prevention and treatment. In 1995, Pelosi succeeded in getting $36 million in AIDS funding cuts restored. She did it in the Appropriations Committee in a move that the *San Francisco Examiner* labeled a "rare victory."[7]

Her victory was the result of a combination of her persuasiveness and of public polls that showed that Americans were, by a margin of 73 percent, in favor of keeping funds for AIDS treatment at current levels or even increasing them.[8]

"It was a very significant thing in that it gave the message to the Republican Congress 'do what you are going to do but don't mess with AIDS funding,'" said Steve Morin.[9]

Even with the Republican Congress, Pelosi started getting more funding for AIDS. By the time President Bill Clinton signed legislation renewing the Ryan White Act for five years, in 1996, the law contained three-quarters of a billion dollars for care of AIDS patients and an additional $50 million for the development of more and better drugs to attack the disease. Pelosi was instrumental in pushing for the additional funding, which was $106 million more than had been allocated in the previous year, a rarity in a year of budget cuts.[10]

"She offered some significant increases in funds amendments which were ultimately agreed to," said Morin. "That, you have to attribute to her political skills. No one could quote believe that we were getting those increases.

"She was persuasive and persistent," he added, naming the two qualities that would be significant in her entire career.[11]

Through the early 2000s, Pelosi kept fighting for more money for AIDS and HIV. She wrote letters to the Department of Health and Human Services, stressing San Francisco's need for funds and clinics. She held hearings both in Washington, D.C., and San Francisco. She worked behind the scenes from her perch on the Appropriations Committee to get funding passed and implemented.

But she was fighting another battle, too. As AIDS spread from major metropolitan areas across the country, other states and cities began to clamor for funds. Senators and Representatives from rural areas began to question the funding formula that directed money to cities like San Francisco. With President George W. Bush in the White House and funds running tight, efforts to redirect more money to other states began to succeed.

Pelosi fought a holding action.

She got a smaller cut than planned in 2000, meaning that San Francisco would lost only 15 percent of its Ryan White money, less than the president and the Republican Congress wanted.

The war on AIDS began branching out after 2000 and became global. And after the September 11, 2001 attacks on New York and Washington, it became a national security problem, as well.

In 2001 and beyond, Pelosi and others continued their crusade to get money to combat AIDS around the world, likening it often to the war on terrorism and noting that in some countries, particularly in Africa, young people were still dying at appalling rates.

The issues had expanded from simple drug therapy in San Francisco to combating AIDS in Africa, where some infected people don't even have the means to tell time, let alone take medication on a regular schedule. Money was all important, and as Pelosi moved into the Speakership, she vowed to do all she could do to fund AIDS care.

Because, as she put it in that emotional speech commemorating the twenty-fifth anniversary of the first official AIDS diagnosis, "How many good friends we held in our arms like bags of bones? Older people, younger people—it's so sad.

"The encouraging thing is that the caregivers were so strong, they never seemed to burn out; and people were determined that there would be a cure, prevention, treatment and a vaccine," she said, the determination in her voice reflecting the words she spoke.[12]

NOTES

1. Venise Wagner, "S.F. Marks AIDS Day by Dedicating Grove: Site in GG Park Becomes National Landmark for 9th Annual Global Event," *San Francisco Examiner,* December 2, 1996, p. A1.

2. Office of Nancy Pelosi, remarks at the U.S. Capitol, April 18, 2007.

3. Nancy Pelosi, speech, June 1, 2006, San Francisco, Calif., Office of Nancy Pelosi.

4. Information is available at www.aidsquilt.org, "Search the Quilt" feature.

5. Steve Morin, interview with author, San Francisco, November 27, 2007.

6. "House Passes AIDS 'Breakthrough' Bill/Money for Cities to Pay for Patient Care," *San Francisco Chronicle,* August 4, 1990, p. A9.

7. Louis Freedberg, "Pelosi Amendment Restores $36 Million in AIDS Funds," *San Francisco Chronicle,* March 2, 1995, p. 2.

8. Ibid.

9. Steve Morin, interview with author, San Francisco, November 27, 2007.

10. Louis Freedberg, "Clinton Signs Bill Renewing AIDS Care; Ryan White Program Extended 5 Years," *San Francisco Chronicle,* May 21, 1996, p. 3.

11. Steve Morin, interview with author, San Francisco, November 27, 2007.

12. Nancy Pelosi, speech, June 1, 2006, San Francisco, Calif., Office of Nancy Pelosi.

Chapter 10

FUNDRAISER

When Nancy Pelosi was a girl in Baltimore, doing her father's political work, the mayor's organization kept track of the things it had done for people in a "favor file," a box of index cards.

Half a century later, the modern equivalent of that index card box was a computerized database of about 30,000 names kept at Democratic headquarters in Washington.

Pelosi built the two files essentially the same way—one name at a time, one request at a time, one donation at a time.

By the time she became Speaker, Pelosi was possibly the biggest single fundraiser the Congress had ever seen. She seemed indefatigable. She canvassed the country to attend fundraisers for other members of Congress. She was on the phone constantly drumming up money. She knew that money meant more Democrats elected to Congress and more Democrats elected to Congress meant more power for her.

For all of her causes—China, AIDS, women's issues, opposition to the war in Iraq—her bedrock cause was raising money.

She came back to that cause again and again, racking up chits and favors as she went. She went all out for Democrats and expected loyalty in return. And if she felt that someone had been disloyal, she could put her immense fundraising network to work against that person.

An example was a race in 2002 in Michigan that pitted the veteran Rep. John Dingell, who had first won his seat in 1955, against Lynn Rivers, a competent but less experienced member of Congress. Pelosi donated $12,000 to Rivers, going against Dingell, who had represented the Detroit area since Pelosi was lining up those index cards in her daddy's favor file.

Dingell fumed at Pelosi's large donation to his opponent but publicly called it a "minor annoyance."

It may have been more than minor, but the Pelosi donation was a drop in the bucket. The Dingell-Rivers race was Michigan's most expensive primary. Dingell raised $2.5 million and Rivers $1.5 million. The race was even through the summer.

But Dingell won the primary, 59 percent to 41 percent.[1]

Pelosi-watchers wrote off her support of Rivers as a political mistake. But she knew exactly what she was doing. Aside from money, the most important thing in politics to Pelosi is loyalty. Rivers had backed her for a leadership post; Dingell had gone against her.

"She was for me. He was not," Pelosi explained succinctly in an interview three years later.[2]

From the beginning of her career, people knew that she could raise money. In her first run for office, Agar Jaicks remembered that people questioned whether she would be a good candidate. His answer: "Pelosi is going to raise the money."[3] She did, and she won.

Jaicks and others remembered that as chairman of the California Democratic Party, she had to raise money to pay the bills, so she did.

In 1984, she had to assure the national Democratic Party that she would raise $3 million to supplement the $6 million the city of San Francisco pledged to underwrite the cost of holding the convention there. She did it and recruited 10,000 volunteers at the same time.

She raised plenty of money in 1986 to help the Democrats recapture the U.S. Senate.

And, in a two-sentence story reporting on her first election, the *New York Times* called her a "Democratic fund-raiser who never before held elected office."[4]

She kept up that fundraising as she progressed through Congress. Once her own seat was secure, after she was re-elected to a full term in 1988, she devoted more and more of her time to helping others raise money.

For example, in 1990, Pelosi cheerfully told her Democratic colleagues that a court in California had lifted the state's limit on campaign contributions. "Good news!" she wrote in a memo, indicating that they could now contribute unlimited amounts to former San Francisco Mayor Dianne Feinstein's first campaign for the Senate.

"Because a challenge can be made to the ruling, we have been advised to get our checks in today," she added, excitement leaping off the page. "Dianne is asking members of the delegation to contribute, or raise, $10, 000 each for the Feinstein for Governor campaign."[5]

Through the 1990s, Pelosi helped Democrats gather money wherever she could. While she was concentrating on building up her reputation in Congress, she was reaching out to other members and asking if she could help them with their fundraising. She worked closely with the Democratic Congressional Campaign Committee, the group that helps Democrats who are running for office.

Her Republican opponents considered her a worthy adversary, and she won their respect, even though they didn't agree with her on issues. At first, the goal was simply to unite Democrats and elect more Democrats. But after the Democrats lost control of the House in 1994, the fundraising became more urgent.

Republican Majority Leader Tom DeLay paid her many high compliments, but none more impressive than when he called her a "worthy opponent." DeLay was a fundraising behemoth for his party—just as Pelosi was for hers.[6]

DeLay and Pelosi also shared another trait—they both took care of the needs of their members. DeLay did it with late-night pizza in his office; Pelosi did it with phone calls, condolence visits, and, yes, late-night meals and snacks in her office during sessions that lasted until the wee hours of the morning or even all night.

But it was the money—always the money—that set her apart. Between 1999 and 2004, Pelosi's Political Action Committee, "PAC to the Future," a committee formed simply to raise and donate money, gave nearly $2.8 million to help Democrats win races across the nation. She raised millions more for the Democratic Party during that time, as well.

She used her personal connections to California millionaires as a basis to build her fundraising. Her donors came from business, industry, and labor. She got money from recognizable names and from unheralded people, as well.

Her donors included members of the Gallo family, makers of wine; the Haas family, heirs to the Levi Strauss Company; the Growald family, Rockefeller family heirs; the Fisher family, owners of the Gap; and the Prizker family, owners of Hyatt Hotels.[7]

She also seemed to have a personal pipeline to the singer/actress Barbra Streisand, for example. In 1986, Streisand gave a concert that raised $1.2 million for Democrats.[8] More than 20 years later, Streisand was still at it, raising $1.3 million for Democrats at her Malibu, California, home at an event that featured Pelosi.[9]

As her efforts to take back the House for Democrats heated up, so did her fundraising. She gathered between $7 million and $8 million for the

2002 campaign and made appearances in 30 states and 90 congressional districts.[10]

She was gunning for a leadership job even then, but her efforts to have the Democrats take back control of the House were unrewarded.

2004 ELECTION

In 2004, when a net gain of 11 seats would have shifted power to her party, Pelosi stepped up the fundraising, traveling to more than 50 cities and raising about $30 million for the Democrats. Unfortunately for her, Republicans kept control, but she continued to build a loyal following among those members of Congress whom she helped.

"If I couldn't raise a dime, people would say, 'What are you bringing to the table?'" she said. "I've shown that I can pull my weight."[11]

She wasn't too fussy about ideology in those days, either. In 2002, she went to help Rep. Paul Kanjorski of Pennsylvania, who was much more conservative than she. Kanjorski, who might have been assumed to not want such a liberal Democratic woman at his side, turned it into an asset, saying her presence showed that he was a "consensus builder."[12]

While doing all this fundraising, Pelosi professed to be a supporter of campaign finance reform, or changing the rules that govern how much money can be raised or spent during campaigns. She generally voted for reforms. But she was not out front in pressing for changes. She had learned to operate too well within the existing rules for that.

She did run afoul of campaign laws at least once and was forced to pay a fine. In 2003, the Federal Election Commission fined Pelosi's PAC $21,000 for improperly accepting donations that exceeded the limit set by federal law.

That PAC was called Team Majority, and it was one of two committees run by Pelosi at that time, the other being PAC to the Future. The federal officials ruled that by using two committees and having people donate to both, she was exceeding the limits on donations set by federal law.

Some of those who got money from the Pelosi PACs also were fined by the federal regulators. Ironically, one of them was Rep. Chris Van Hollen of Maryland, who years later would be tapped by Pelosi to run the Democrats' campaign committee.

Those who have seen her operate as a fundraiser say she is smooth as silk but forceful at the same time. She is so committed and sincere about her efforts that people just open their wallets and give. She is tough, too, and tells people that if they want to make a difference in politics, they have to put their money up.

Cressey Nakagawa, a San Francisco attorney and Democratic Party activist who knew Pelosi for 35 years, said part of her appeal was that while she could tap the wealthy for big bucks, she mingled well with ordinary people, too. "She could put a hand on your shoulder and you'd write a check," he said, smiling at the thought of her deft touch and her ability to always, always remember names.[13]

"She really does have that magic touch," Nakagawa added.[14]

Throughout it all, Pelosi professed not to like raising money all that much. "I hate it," she claimed in 2006.

But she knew where her talents were.

"I admit this, I am good at it. I listen to people and I know what they are interested in. So I don't waste their time," she said.[15]

Pelosi continued her fundraising efforts even after becoming Speaker. She went to Laredo, Texas, to help out Rep. Henry Cuellar, in one of the poorest places in the nation. She held a Washington fundraiser for Melissa Bean, of Illinois, who had wrested a seat from a Republican. And she went to Boston to host a fundraiser in 2007 for Niki Tsongas, who was running in a special election, not unlike the one Pelosi had run in back in 1987. Pelosi knew all too well that special elections are tricky animals that require a combination of luck, talent, and, yes, money.

She also knew that by traveling the country far and wide in search of funds for Democrats, she was building up a "favor file" that she would need as she tried to move up the ladder into leadership that would eventually take her to the highest congressional post in the nation.

NOTES

1. Almanac of American Politics, online version, June 22, 2005 update; available at http://nationaljournal.com/pubs/almanac/2006/people/mi/rep_mi15.htm.

2. Marc Sandalow and Erin McCormick, "Pelosi's Goal: Democrats Back on Top; Minority Leader Practices Hardball Politics to Position Her Party for Midterm Election," San Francisco Chronicle, April 2, 2006, p. 1.

3. Agar Jaicks, interview with author, October 18, 2007.

4. Associated Press, "Congresswoman Sworn In," New York Times, June 11, 1987.

5. Susan Yoachum, Greg Lucas, and Jerry Roberts, "Campaign Financing, Pelosi Hurries to Raise Funds for Feinstein," San Francisco Chronicle, October 2, 1990, p. A7.

6. David Von Drehle and Hanna Rosin, "The Two Nancy Pelosis; New House Leader Stresses Her Political Skills," Washington Post, November 14, 2002, p. A1.

7. Erin McCormick and Mark Sandalow, "Pelosi Mines 'California Gold' for Dems Nationwide; Personal Skills, Wide Network of Wealthy Donors Help Party's House Leader Gather Millions," San Francisco Chronicle, April 3, 2006, p. 1.

8. ABC News, "Streisand Hosts Pelosi at Fundraiser," April 13, 2007.

9. Ibid.

10. David Von Drehle and Hanna Rosin, "The Two Nancy Pelosis; New House Leader Stresses Her Political Skills," *Washington Post*, November 14, 2002, p. A1.

11. Louis Freedberg, "Pelosi Raises Big War Chest for Democrats; $3 Million in Donations Boosts S.F. Liberal's Bid for a Top House Position," *San Francisco Chronicle*, October 14, 2000, p. A1.

12. David Von Drehle and Hanna Rosin, "The Two Nancy Pelosis; New House Leader Stresses Her Political Skills," *Washington Post*, November 14, 2002, p. A1.

13. Cressey H. Nakagawa, interview with author, San Francisco, November 8, 2007.

14. Cressey H. Nakawawa, interview with author, San Francisco, December 10, 2007.

15. Erin McCormick and Mark Sandalow, "Pelosi Mines 'California Gold' for Dems Nationwide; Personal Skills, Wide Network of Wealthy Donors Help Party's House Leader Gather Millions," *San Francisco Chronicle*, April 3, 2006, p. 1.

Chapter 11

KEEPING SECRETS

There are many rooms in the Capitol that are off limits to the public, but at least two of them stand out as being sealed off not only to the public but to most of those who work on Capitol Hill as well. One is in the basement, the other in the attic. Nancy Pelosi has spent a considerable amount of time in both.

The basement room sits just to the right of the large doors that open up onto the Mall side of the Capitol. Surrounded by custodial workrooms and the office that is responsible for distributing flags that are flown over the Capitol each day, the room is entered through a heavy but nondescript door that reads, "Committee on Standards of Official Conduct." In other words, it's the Ethics Committee, the panel in charge of investigating wrongdoing by members of Congress.

The attic room is even more secluded. Reachable only by a special elevator or a guarded set of stairs, it is the meeting place of the Select Committee on Intelligence, which deals with international spying and "black box" operations around the world. Members who sit in that room are privy to secrets that, if revealed, could endanger the security of the nation, not to mention the welfare of American spies.

Pelosi spent 10 years on the Intelligence Committee, from 1995 through 2006, the longest continuous period of service in the committee's history. Once she moved into the House leadership, she became an unofficial member of the committee, but she still attended its secret sessions. Her experience would prove invaluable after the September 11, 2001, attacks and during the Iraq War.

Together, Pelosi's service on the two panels indicate the trust that other members of the House had in her and her ability to use her judgment and discretion to deal with the most sensitive matters. It also highlighted her behind-the-scenes skills. By taking a position on the Ethics Committee, a job that not many other members wanted, she knew that they would be grateful to her, as long as she was perceived as fair. She was building up her chits with other members in this way.

And by sitting on Intelligence, where she was prohibited from talking publicly about what she knew, Pelosi would become a private resource for other members of Congress seeking guidance when making decisions on sensitive matters. While Pelosi was not able to disclose the nation's secrets to them, she could guide them in their thought process without compromising intelligence.

The Ethics Committee is responsible for upholding the rules that govern actions of members of Congress. That means that members of the Ethics Committee resemble the Internal Affairs offices in police departments, they look into misbehavior by House members and figure out what punishments to hand out. Understandably, given the nature of the job, it's not a very popular post. House members would rather be handing out plums on the Appropriations Committee or writing tax law or dealing with health and welfare—anything but policing their fellow Congress members. In addition to being an unpopular position, members of the Ethics Committee should be above reproach themselves.

Nancy Pelosi served on the Ethics Committee from February 1991 to January 1997—a long stretch for any member of that panel. And Pelosi's tenure encompassed some of the most difficult and taxing ethics cases to face the committee.

Ironically, her personal career got a bit of a boost because of the ethical problems of a colleague. In 1992, Rep. Mary Rose Oakar, a Cleveland Democrat, got caught up in the House Bank scandal. For a long time, the House had its own bank, which served members of Congress just like a regular bank, but with looser rules. That scandal involved members of Congress who wrote checks on the House bank for which they did not have enough money in the bank to cover the amount. They counted on the bank to cover their checks. Oakar was found to have written 213 overdrafts. Concerned about appearances, the Democratic Party decided to remove Oakar as the head of the party's platform committee for the 1992 convention. Nancy Pelosi got the job and another highly visible party position.

The most difficult case that the Ethics Committee had to deal with during Pelosi's tenure involved former House Speaker Newt Gingrich, a

Georgia Republican. Gingrich was a divisive figure, who had come to power by stressing that the "old style" of Republicans and their "get along, go along" philosophy of dealing with Democrats was outdated and unproductive. He had a "take no prisoners" style, stressed Republican Party differences with Democrats, and demanded loyalty from his own party. He ran roughshod over many Democrats—he said he was simply emulating the treatment Democrats had given him—but he left nerve endings frayed.

Gingrich claimed some successes. He successfully brought the Republicans to power in the 1994 elections, overcoming 40 years of Democratic rule in the House. He set up the "Contract with America" as the overarching theme for Republicans running for Congress that year, overturning a long tradition in which mostly local issues formed the cornerstone of congressional campaigns.

The "Contract with America" called for a balanced-budget constitutional amendment; term limits for members of Congress; restitution for crime victims; the line-item veto, which would allow presidents to veto individual items in Congress bills; conversion of the federal welfare program to 50 programs run by the states; tax cuts; and changes to House rules to limit the power of committee chairmen.[1] The public bought it, electing 52 more Republicans in the House and handing the chamber to the Republicans, a state that would not be reversed until Pelosi became Speaker 12 years later.

Many of the changes the House had endorsed did not survive the Senate or President Bill Clinton's veto pen, but they cemented Gingrich's control over the House.

However, Gingrich had made enemies. There was animosity on the part of Democrats who harbored resentment against Gingrich for filing ethics charges against former Speaker Jim Wright, a Texas Democrat. Wright was forced to resign as Speaker in 1989, after the Ethics Committee reported that he had used bulk purchases of his book, *Reflections of a Public Man*, to earn speaking fees in excess of what was allowed under House rules at the time, and that his wife, Betty, was given a sham job to avoid the House's limits on outside income earnings by members of Congress.

In the four years that Gingrich served as Speaker, from 1995 to 1999, an astounding 84 ethics charges were filed against him, including one charge that he claimed tax-exempt status for a college course he taught. Gingrich was reprimanded and fined $300,000 by the Ethics Committee, the largest fine ever levied by the panel, after investigators found that he had supplied inaccurate information to the panel, representing an "intentional or...reckless" disregard of House rules. Special Counsel James M. Cole concluded that Gingrich violated federal tax law and had lied to the ethics panel in an effort to force the committee to dismiss the complaint against him. The House upheld the charges on an overwhelming vote, making Gingrich the first Speaker in the 208-year history of the House to be so disciplined.[2]

The 395-28 vote closed the door on a tumultuous episode that had begun when former Rep. Ben Jones, a Georgia Democrat who was then running against Gingrich, filed the first ethics complaint. When Republicans took the House in the 1994 elections and Gingrich became Speaker, the ethics situation became more intense. In 1996 and 1998, Democrats tried to get the House back, unsuccessfully. As the charges mounted against Gingrich, and Democrats felt they could use the Speaker's problems to their advantage, the partisan strains in the House intensified.

Pelosi, muzzled because of her position on the Ethics Committee, couldn't say much during the Gingrich case. But the partisanship obviously bothered her. She was also outraged at his lying to his fellow members of Congress. She said it was a violation of trust. "We trust each other that we will deal truthfully with each other," she said on the day Gingrich was sanctioned.[3]

But the next day, her six-year tenure on the panel having almost come to an end, Pelosi felt free to vent a bit about what that case meant to her. She called it an "awful" experience and said that Gingrich manipulated the process from start to finish, first by calling the shots for the Ethics Committee chairwoman, Nancy Johnson, a Connecticut Republican, and then by indicating to other Republicans that the charges were not that serious.

From Pelosi's perspective, the secret hearings into the Gingrich case were so sensitive that she once had to ask her husband, Paul, to leave their bedroom at 3 A.M. so that she could take a private phone call on the situation. For her, Gingrich's transgressions were very serious, serious enough for him to step aside as Speaker. But the Republicans wanted to protect him, so they advocated the fine and reprimand. Pelosi said it wasn't worth it to make more out of the case; the damage had already been done.[4]

But she served notice that she believed Republicans should replace him as Speaker. "He is technically eligible," she said. "I hope you will make a judgment as to whether he is ethically fit."[5]

No matter, the Republicans kept Gingrich on. But after Republicans did poorly in the elections of 1998, he resigned from the Speakership and from his seat in Congress.

The Gingrich case was certainly the most sensational of Pelosi's service on the Ethics Committee, but it was by no means the only difficult and embarrassing case for Congress while she was there.

In 1995, for example, Rep. Mel Reynolds, a Chicago Democrat, re-signed his seat after the panel opened an inquiry into allegations that he had misused his staff for personal purposes and failed to pay his debts. He also was convicted in state court of solicitation of an underage girl. The incident was particularly embarrassing for Congress, as Reynolds, a relative newcomer, had been touted as a man on the rise and had been shepherded to plum committee assignments by much more senior members.

Then there was the case of Rep. Charlie Wilson, a Texas Democrat who was known as "Good Time Charlie." Wilson was a flamboyant type, who generally squired around at least one attractive woman, if not two, at the same time. He always said that as a single man, he was doing nothing wrong. He also took up the cause of the Afghan rebels, known as the Mujahadeen, who were fighting against the Soviet Union in Afghanistan. Wilson personally saw to it that the "Muj," as he called them, were well armed. He even fought alongside them a couple of times. Most in Congress were willing to put up with his extreme behavior, because he was a pretty good congressman in general. But when he was accused of improper use of campaign funds and inadequate financial disclosure, in late 1995, the Ethics Committee was called into action. An investigation ensued. Wilson's campaign paid a $90,000 fine to the Federal Election Commission, and he was "admonished" by the committee to make sure that he adhered to campaign finance rules and all other rules of the House.[6]

The committee barely got to touch the case of Rep. Dan Rostenkowski, an Illinois Democrat, who was indicted for mail fraud, wire fraud, witness tampering, making false statements and embezzlement, revolving around a case against him for misusing postage stamps and office furniture. He was defeated for re-election in November 1994, before the committee could take action. He later served time in jail.[7]

These were the unsavory sorts of things that Pelosi got to deal with on the Ethics Committee. It was no wonder that she was happy to be relieved of that duty.

INTELLIGENCE COMMITTEE

The Intelligence Committee was another kind of secret panel. This time, Pelosi was dealing with the most sensitive information a member of Congress is allowed to see. As an indication of how secret the panel's deliberations are, its meetings are not listed on the schedules for Congress, and members don't talk about what they do there. Often, the only way to know that the Intelligence Committee has met is to watch if one of the members comes out of a special elevator. Even then, their purposes for being on that elevator are unknown.

From 1995 until she became Speaker, in 2007, Pelosi issued no press releases about her intelligence work. She did not discuss it in speeches. But the knowledge that she gained from serving on that committee would prove invaluable after the September 11, 2001, terrorist attacks on the United States and in her dealings with the war in Iraq.

In 1998, as a member of the Intelligence Committee, she did burst briefly into public view on secret matters when she went with a delegation of lawmakers to Guatemala to investigate the assassination of an activist bishop, Juan Jose Gerardi, head of the Human Rights Center of Guatemalan Archbishops. Gerardi was bludgeoned to death with a concrete block after he released a report blaming government forces and death squads for human rights violations during a 35-year civil war in Guatemala.[8]

Pelosi and Rep. George Miller, another California Democrat and Pelosi's close colleague, traveled to Guatemala to look into it. She went to the country's Defense Ministry, a scary-looking place right out of a movie. Amid the guns and bodyguards, the defense minister started to spin a tale that had little bearing on the truth. Pelosi was having none of it. "I've been on the Intelligence Committee for...years," she snapped. "I have this pain in my back from reading thousands of pages of transcripts about what's happened down here. So don't even say that." The minister was taken aback.[9]

Her dealings with the Chinese also steeled her resolve to be tough with foreign governments that were abusing their power.

In 1999, the "Cox Committee" released a report documenting the counterintelligence failures of the U.S. government over the previous two decades and concluded that espionage efforts by the Chinese, particularly in stealing American technology, were continuing. Pelosi said that as a member of the committee she was aware of the "full nature and extent" of the findings, which indicated that the classified information was even more damning than what had been released in public. It cemented Pelosi's notion that the Chinese were not to be trusted.[10]

By the time Al Qaeda terrorists attacked the United States in September 2001, Pelosi probably knew more than anyone about terrorist threats. But she was restrained from saying anything about it publicly, or even privately to most other people. It may not have been as surprising to her as it was to others that the terrorists attacked, but she was as devastated as anyone alive in the nation at that time.

She called the attacks "worse than Pearl Harbor [i.e., the Japanese attack on the United States in 1941 in Hawaii]. There are more civilians. It's right in the heart of our country."

And, knowingly, she added that the attacks have "all the earmarks and all the fingermarks of Osama bin Laden."[11]

Pelosi supported the retaliatory attacks on Afghanistan in response to the 9/11 attacks on the United States. But the war in Iraq was a different story.

Pelosi was given all of the information, classified and unclassified, that the Bush administration was using to support its decision to go to war in Iraq. She, more than most people, understood the basis for the war. She, more than most, had information that was available only to a select few. A majority of the Congress opted to support President George W. Bush's decision to commit American troops to Iraq in an effort to, as he said, protect America against terrorism and to keep Saddam Hussein from acquiring weapons of mass destruction, such as nuclear, chemical, and biological weapons. The Bush administration produced "evidence" that it said made its case. But some, including Pelosi, were skeptical.

She cited her 10 years on the Intelligence Committee in calling for further negotiations instead of war. She said that going to war in Iraq threatened the coalition of nations that had formed to fight terrorism in Iraq. She said that going to war in Iraq might provoke Saddam Hussein to use chemical or biological weapons against American troops, whereas he might not use them if he were not invaded. And she predicted, correctly as it turned out, that the war would be long and could cost hundreds of billions of dollars.

As the night turned into the early hours of the morning that day, Pelosi said that going to war would "show our power to Saddam Hussein. If we resolve this issue diplomatically, we can show our strength as a great country. Let us show our greatness. Vote no on this resolution."[12]

But the Congress, led by House Minority Leader Richard Gephardt, a Missouri Democrat, backed Bush and voted 296–133 in the House and 77–23 in the Senate (at 1:15 A.M.) to give the president the authority to take the nation to war in Iraq.

Years later, when many Democrats who had supported the war changed their minds and said that they had made a mistake by supporting it in the first place, Pelosi could be satisfied in her own mind that she had done the right thing.

The vote was not the last of the Iraq war for Pelosi; far from it. In fact, it would continue to play a major role in her political life and would set her up for her next big step.

Four years later, in a pitched battle with President Bush and the Republicans over control of the House of Representatives, Pelosi would strike back at charges that she was not prepared to deal with the terrorist threat.

"As a mother and grandmother with 14 years on the Intelligence Committee, don't tell me I don't understand what the threat to our country is,"
she snapped at the CBS interviewer Lesley Stahl, when Stahl brought
up Bush's charges that she was unprepared.[13]

It was the kind of steely resolve that those close to Pelosi were used to
seeing. The rest of the country was about to see it, too.

NOTES

1. Ron Elving, "Congress, 10 Years after the Gingrich Revolution," National
Public Radio, January 11, 2005.

2. John E. Yang, "House Reprimands, Penalizes Speaker," *Washington Post*,
January 22, 1997, p. A1.

3. Ibid.

4. Marc Sandalow, "Pelosi Says GOP 'Sandbagged' Gingrich Ethics Investigation; She Says House Speaker Is Unfit for the Job," *San Francisco Chronicle*,
January 23, 1997, p.A1.

5. David Espo, "House Punishes Gingrich," Associated Press release, January 21, 1997.

6. House Ethics Committee Web site, Historical Chart, available at www.
house.gov/ethics/Historical_chart_Final_Version.htm.

7. Ibid.

8. Terrorfile online, The assassination of Bishop Juan Jose Gerardi, available
at http://www.terrorfileonline.org/en/index.php/The_Assassination_of_Bishop_
Juan_Jose_Gerardi.

9. Harold Meyerson, "How Nancy Pelosi Took Control: The San Francisco
Liberal Turns Out to Be a Tough Customer," *The American Prospect*, May 12,
2004. Available at: http://findarticles.com/p/articles/.

10. Office of Rep. Nancy Pelosi, "Statement on the Release of the Cox Committee Report," May 25, 1999.

11. Carolyn Lochhead, "Terror Strikes Deep into Heart of America's Capital;
Ghastly Events Prompt Talk of All-Out War," *San Francisco Chronicle*, September 12, 2001, p. A11.

12. Congressional Record, October 10, 2002, p. H7780.

13. Lesley Stahl, CBS, *60 Minutes,* interview, October 22, 2006.

Seven-year-old Nancy D'Alesandro holds the Bible as her father, Thomas D'Alesandro, Jr., is sworn in as Mayor of Baltimore in May 1947. (Family photo, courtesy Office of Nancy Pelosi)

The D'Alesandro family. Nancy and her mother, Annunciata, are on either side of her father, Thomas D'Alesandro, Jr. Her brothers, left to right: Tommy III, Franklin Roosevelt (Roosey), Nicky (in glasses), Hector, and Joseph. (Courtesy Office of Nancy Pelosi)

Nancy D'Alesandro's formal senior portrait at Trinity College. (Courtesy Trinity, Washington, D.C.)

A teenage Nancy D'Alesandro meets Senator and future president John F. Kennedy. (Courtesy Office of Nancy Pelosi)

Nancy Pelosi during her first run for the
House in 1987. John Burton is in the background. (AP Images)

Newly elected Rep. Nancy Pelosi is sworn in by House
Speaker Jim Wright in 1987. Her father is seated in the
wheelchair; her mother is partially obscured by Wright's
hand. (AP Images)

Nancy and Paul Pelosi admire grandchild number six, Paul Michael Vos, born hours after the election in 2006 that would make her Speaker of the House. (Courtesy Office of Nancy Pelosi)

Speaker of the House-elect Nancy Pelosi meets with President George W. Bush. The two will battle over funding of domestic programs and the war in Iraq. (AP Images)

Speaker of the House Nancy Pelosi surrounded by her grandchildren and the children and grandchildren of other members of the House after she is formally elected speaker, January 4, 2007. (AP Images)

Chapter 12

THE WHIP RACE

Within the halls of Congress, politics is like a three-dimensional chess game; every move is thought out carefully, often far in advance. And every move is weighed against a countermove an opponent might make. Advance planning is critical. But planning too far in advance can upset some people who might be critical to the next move, or the one after that.

By 1998, more than a decade after she was elected to Congress as a neophyte lawmaker, Nancy Pelosi had figured out how to navigate the halls of the Capitol and how to get help for her constituents and the causes she believed in. She had figured out how to help her colleagues with fundraising. She had learned how to discipline unruly members from her perch on the Ethics Committee and how to keep secrets on the Intelligence Committee. She had mastered the money system of the Appropriations Committee.

But her biggest challenge, the one that would put her on the path to making history, was still to come. She had begun to have thoughts of moving into the leadership of the Democratic Party in the House of Representatives.

There is no more complicated maneuver than trying to become a leader in Congress. For both parties, these races are Byzantine in their complexity. In some ways, they are popularity contests like that for high school class president, with the person who gets along the best with the most people having an advantage. But, more important, these contests are like auctions, with all members of the party trying to figure out which candidate will give them the best deal—which one will campaign for them, which one will fundraise for them, which one will give them a better committee assignment, which one will push their cause.

By the time Pelosi was considering running for minority whip, the second highest post when Democrats were in the minority, 215 Democratic members of Congress held the key. Pelosi had campaigned for about 90 of them. She would need 108 to win. She knew all of them. Each had an opinion of her. They all knew that if they pledged their vote to her, they would be in a position to get something in return.

Unlike all other votes in the House of Representatives, ballots for congressional leadership are secret. It's not unusual for members to tell more than one candidate they will vote for them. It's not going too far to say that sometimes, they don't tell the truth. And because the voting is secret, no one will ever know.

Pelosi's mentor, and the man whose seat she filled in Congress, Phil Burton, learned that fact the hard way decades earlier. In 1976, Burton was sure he was in a position to be majority leader, the next step up from whip. He had counted votes, and on the Sunday before the secret election was to take place, he shrugged off the suggestion that some of those who had pledged their votes to him might be lying.

When the voting began in what was then a four-person race, Burton won on the first ballot. Leadership election rules say that if there are more than two candidates in the race, the one with the lowest vote total drops out and a new vote is conducted with the remaining candidates. Burton also won the second round, eliminating another contestant. That left Burton and Rep. Jim Wright from Texas to compete head-to-head for the Democratic whip's job. It turned out that Burton's count was off by one vote; Wright won 148–147 and went on to become Speaker of the House in 1987, the year Pelosi was first elected.

Nancy Pelosi decided to tackle this unforgiving and complicated system with the single purpose of becoming Democratic whip. "Whip" is a term derived from the British and comes, originally, from foxhunting. The whip or "whipper in" was the term for the person who kept the hounds from leaving the pack during a foxhunt. In the modern U.S. House, as in the British Parliament, the whip keeps track of members, counts votes, makes sure members are on hand for votes, and distributes information to party members.

But the whip is more than that. The whip is one of the faces of the party, the person who often speaks for the party. Very often, that person is on television or otherwise in the media as the spokesman for the party. By choosing a whip, a party is making a statement about how it wants to be perceived by the world outside Congress.

No woman had ever held that position before. The "face" of Congress, no matter which party, was always a male face.

When Pelosi first started thinking about running for whip in 1998, Democrats were still in the minority, but Pelosi was optimistic that they could wrest control of the House from the Republicans in the elections of 2000. If that happened, the most likely scenario was that the minority leader, Rep. Richard Gephardt of Missouri, would move up to speaker; Rep. David Bonior of Michigan, the whip a the time, would then move up to majority leader, leaving the whip's spot open.

Another complex scenario involved redistricting. Every 10 years, states draw new congressional districts based on population as determined by the census. All congressional districts must contain approximately the same number of people. That means that states that lose population in the census often lose representatives, and states that gain population often gain representatives. The redistricting process is usually handled by state legislatures and is very political, with the party that is in charge of a state's legislature or governorship attempting to draw the districts to favor itself. But in the end, the number of people in a state determines whether they lose or gain seats in the House of Representatives.

California, for instance, has steadily gained seats through the twentieth and twenty-first centuries, while states in the industrial Northeast have lost population and House seats.

By 1998, it appeared that Bonior might be in danger of losing his seat in Michigan due to redistricting. Michigan's population was down, and the early betting was that Bonior might have to run against another sitting member of Congress from Michigan or choose to seek another office. That scenario, too, would lead to an open whip's job.

There was another factor at work in Pelosi's mind, as well. She was tired of Democrats being in the minority in the House. She was also fed up with what she viewed as the complacency of Democratic leaders. She didn't see the ingredients necessary to take back the House under the current leadership. She wouldn't confront or condemn any of the current leaders, not even in public. That wasn't her style. She figured the best thing to do was get moving on her own to break into leadership and change things from there.[1]

Without consulting Bonior or Gephardt, Pelosi began quietly to make plans. She did a quick survey of the Congress to see if she could attract 80 votes, the number that she thought she needed just as a base, to put her in contention for the job. She was pleased to find that many people initially said they would support her.

By 1999, the planning was in earnest. She held a small dinner with a few loyal members of Congress whom she intended to put on her "whip team." They were on board.

Pelosi was still thinking that the Democrats might win the House back in the elections of 2000. Former Vice President Al Gore was running for president on the Democratic side, and the initial betting was that he would win because George W. Bush, the Republican candidate, was not perceived to be that strong and Gore was supposed to carry on the successful economic mandate of Bill Clinton.

She started running for whip on that basis.

Two rivals caught wind of Pelosi's moves and weren't happy. Rep. Steny Hoyer of Maryland, Pelosi's old friend from their days as interns in Maryland Sen. Daniel Brewster's office decades earlier, thought he was in a position to move up to whip. Hoyer's career had been a long, slow, steady climb up the ladder. After the stint in Brewster's office, he was elected to the Maryland State Senate in 1966 at age 27, just after graduating from law school. He became state Senate president in 1975 at age 35, the youngest ever to hold the job. He ran unsuccessfully for lieutenant governor of Maryland in 1978, but then, when former Rep. Gladys Noon Spellman of Maryland fell ill and gave up the seat, he won a special election for Congress in 1981, beating Spellman's husband and several other candidates.

By 1989, Hoyer had become chairman of the House Democratic Caucus, one step below whip in the leadership hierarchy. He tried to grab the whip's job in 1991, when Democrats still controlled the House, but was badly beaten by Bonior, who had corralled the "old bulls" in the House and gotten them to round up votes for him. Bonior won, 160–109. Hoyer then served in a number of lesser leadership-type posts, biding his time and waiting for the next obvious opening.

The other whip candidate was equally miffed by Pelosi's running start at the job. Rep. John Lewis of Georgia was a veteran of the 1960s civil rights movement who worked with the Rev. Martin Luther King. He was widely regarded as a leading "moral" voice on Capitol Hill—his wisdom born of experience, and a couple of serious cracks in his skull at the hands of overzealous law enforcement officers during the civil rights marches in the South. With his deep voice and a bearing reflecting the preacher that he was before going into politics, he commanded respect and attention. When he rose on the House floor to oppose the impeachment of President Bill Clinton in 1998, his preacher's cadence soaring through the chamber, even Republicans stopped talking to listen to him.

In 1998, Lewis wrote a biography, *Walking with the Wind*, about his experiences in the civil rights movement and beyond. He traveled the country promoting the book and also worked to gain support for a potential run for whip. In 1999, he was serving as one of four chief deputy Democratic whips, with the whip post the next step up.

In August 1999, having already expressed his dismay to Pelosi and others that the race was starting so early, Lewis declared he was running for whip. He, too, organized dinners around his candidacy and started drumming up support. But he found it tough going and was particularly upset when one of his natural supporters, Rep. Cynthia McKinney, also from Georgia and also African American, held a dinner for Pelosi. McKinney said she did not know Lewis wanted the job.[2]

Lewis wasn't the only one to feel betrayed. Pelosi had her problems, too. Rep. Ellen Tauscher, a California Democrat from Contra Costa, decided to support Hoyer, the only member of the California delegation to do so. News stories at the time indicated that Pelosi's allies in Sacramento might make Tauscher's life difficult by redrawing her congressional district in a way that would be less favorable to her—probably one that contained fewer of her natural supporters. Pelosi denied that was going on, but the feud between Pelosi and Tauscher simmered.

[By September 2001, Tauscher's fear had come true. Her district was redrawn by the California legislature to include four counties, not the original two, and included some more liberal Democratic areas, where voters were not predisposed to support Tauscher. Senate President Pro-Tem John Burton, Pelosi's close ally and brother of Phil Burton, denied that the district was redrawn as payback.[3]]

Meanwhile, Hoyer was also holding dinners and soliciting support. The competing dinners, campaigning, and vote-courting went on for months. As 1999 turned into 2000 and the presidential and congressional election campaigns began in earnest, the whip race became a marathon. It began to get to be too much for Lewis, who was also criss-crossing the country promoting his book at the same time.

At about midyear, Lewis decided he'd had enough. He sought out Hoyer to throw his support to the Marylander in return for some promises to place African Americans and other minorities on key committees. Hoyer told Lewis he was going to win.[4]

And that's how it looked to Hoyer and many of the outsiders evaluating the race that summer. But despite Lewis's endorsement of Hoyer, Pelosi kept pushing, expecting some of the members of the Black Caucus to endorse her eventually. It was that "face" thing again, she figured; the African Americans would be more inclined to vote for a fresh face.

At the same time, she was aggressively recruiting Democrats to run for Congress, in her effort to mold a Democratic majority. A case in point: In late 1999, Pelosi sat down with former Rep. Jane Harman, a Democrat from southern California, who had given up her House seat two years before to mount an unsuccessful bid for governor. Pelosi wanted

Harman to jump back into politics again and try to get her old congressional seat back. Harman, exhausted and discouraged from her failed campaign, was hesitant. Pelosi talked her into it, using a combination of personal persuasion and a couple of big carrots. If Harmon won, Pelosi said, she'd get her seniority back and a seat on a plum committee. Harmon agreed and made the race about Democrats taking back the House, arguing that "it matters who leads Congress."[5] It was a squeaker, but Harmon pulled off the victory against Republican Steven Kuykendall, who had succeeded her.[6]

Harmon got a spot on the prestigious Energy and Commerce Committee and a seat on the Intelligence Committee. In later years, Harmon and Pelosi would clash over the Intelligence Panel, but in 2000, it was all smiles between them.

The Harmon race was just one of about half a dozen that Pelosi threw herself into in California in 2000, hoping that her efforts would be enough to win the House and herself the whip job. She called on her experiences in the past to mount huge volunteer organizations to work on the Democratic campaigns in California, just as she had done for herself back in 1987. Rep. George Miller, who represented the district next to Pelosi's in San Francisco and who was one of her closest confidants, said Pelosi told each Democratic candidate in that state that if he or she didn't have 1,000 volunteers on the ground, no one should even think of calling on Pelosi for help.[7]

But if the candidates did meet Pelosi's standards, they got plenty of help. In addition to working with members and candidates from California, Pelosi's network was stretching nationwide. She gave $25,000 to Rep. Brad Carson, a Rhodes Scholar from Oklahoma, who attracted both Pelosi's and Hoyer's attention when he was first running in 1998. After he won, he kept getting more attention from the two. They eventually gave him $50,000 combined, and split evenly between them. They were both looking for his vote for whip. Carson accepted all of the money but didn't tip his hand to which of them he would support for whip. Eventually he would support Hoyer. But Hoyer was finding it difficult to compete with Pelosi, dollar for dollar. Pelosi could tap the vast resources of rich folks in Northern California for her cash. Hoyer's middle-class district outside Washington was made up mostly of government workers. He didn't have the natural fundraising base that she had.

By the time the 2000 elections arrived, Hoyer had raised only $1.5 million to Pelosi's $3.9 million, a staggering sum for a whip race.

But it wasn't enough. In the 2000 elections, Democrats gained seats in the House, including five in California (Pelosi played a prominent role in all of them, including Harman's), but their wins overall were not enough to capture the majority.

The 2000 presidential election also was the most bizarre in American history, with Gov. George W. Bush of Texas, the Republican nominee, and Vice President Al Gore, the Democrat, essentially deadlocked. That election was not over on election night, nor the day after, nor the day after that. It came down to a contest of who had won Florida, an essential swing state. Recounts were started and stopped; both sides went to court in Florida, and the Florida Supreme Court said the recounts could continue. Eventually, the contest ended up in the Supreme Court, which stopped the recount in Florida with a ruling on December 12 that said that the Florida court had improperly set a new standard for counting votes. With the recount stopped, Florida went to Bush, giving Bush the victory with the most electoral votes, 271–266, though Gore had won more of the popular votes overall, with 50,996,583 for Gore and 50,456,062 for Bush. Along with the failure to capture Congress, the presidential election was a crushing blow to Democrats.[8]

Though disappointed, Pelosi was undeterred. She immediately went to work for the next election cycle, figuring that, having gotten close in 2000, the Democrats would carry the day in the next election, in 2002.

But, for her own political ambitions, it turned out she didn't have to wait that long. As expected, Rep. David Bonior, the minority whip, got caught in redistricting and decided by early 2001 to run for governor rather than fight another incumbent for his House seat. The whip race was on again.

Through the spring and summer, Hoyer and Pelosi kept up their contest. With 215 Democrats in the House, each knew it would take 108 to win. Many House members had declared their intent to support one or the other early on. The race focused on about 20 or so members who had been publicly undecided.

Pelosi pulled out all the stops. One day during Congress's summer recess, months before the whip election would take place, Rep. Cal Dooley, a California Democrat, stopped by his office to check messages. Rifling through the usual slips of paper, one jumped out at him: Ernest Gallo, the famed California winemaker, wanted to talk to him. Though a loyal member of the House's "Wine Caucus," made up of members who have wine manufacturers in their states, Dooley had never talked to Gallo. He called back.

Gallo wanted to talk about Pelosi and to say that electing a whip from California would be good for both of them. Dooley, more conservative than Pelosi, had close ties with Hoyer. But how could he say no to Gallo, the elder statesman of American wine and a man important to Dooley's constituents in California?

He told Gallo he'd think about it.[9]

As summer turned into fall, Congress was back in session, and Pelosi and Hoyer kept piling up the votes. Hoyer said he had 100 commitments; Pelosi said she had 120. The only problem was that the total was more than the 215 Democrats in the House. Someone—possibly several someones—wasn't telling the truth.

Bonior was getting ready to publicly announce that he was resigning as whip so he could run for governor of Michigan. He readied a statement for September 11, 2001. But that statement never got delivered. That morning, two planes slammed into the World Trade Center in New York, another hit the Pentagon, just across the Potomac River from the Capitol, and a fourth crashed in a field in Pennsylvania. The worst terrorist attack on American soil had taken place that day. Nothing much else mattered.

Pelosi, a member of the House Intelligence Committee, got a secret briefing on the attacks. Congress was recessed for the day, but Pelosi and most other members of Congress stressed they were eager to go back to work.

After a decent interval of about two weeks, the race for whip resumed, pointing to an Oct. 10 vote. The crusty veteran Rep. John Dingell, D-Mich., was in Hoyer's camp and tried to woo wavering Democrats. Pelosi's team worked just as hard and countered with equally seasoned Rep. John Murtha of Pennsylvania, who appealed to a more conservative wing of the party.

Former Rep. Sam Gejdensen of Connecticut was on Pelosi's team. He remembered that no one got out of the way for Pelosi; no one smoothed the way for her. It was her tireless work, personal grace, understanding of the political process, and savvy politicking that all worked together. And, of course, her not taking anything for granted, even a pledge for a vote.

"We went over the lists," said Gejdensen. "We didn't count people who said nice things to us, we counted people who said yes, publicly, and said I will sign a letter and say I am for you."[10]

Hoyer was counting, too, and running hard, leading to some animosity between the two. Hoyer refuses to call it a bitter rivalry. Rather, he said it's almost impossible to run against another member for so long without some "elbows out."[11]

The relationship between Hoyer and Pelosi was long and complicated: They were united by party, divided by philosophy (he was more conservative, though not by much); united by home state (Maryland), divided by ambition.

Neither gave ground in the whip competition. But as the vote got closer, Pelosi appeared to be pulling ahead, thanks to her dogged work and the fact that the idea of a woman in leadership had begun to be appealing to Democrats.

On the day of the voting, Pelosi and her team left nothing to chance. They rounded up supporters from as far away as Guam. Guam's delegate to Congress doesn't get to vote on regular issues, but as a Democrat, he could vote in Democratic caucus and in the whip race. He had a funeral to attend in the middle of the Pacific the day before, but he flew all night, changed planes four times, crossed countless time zones, and made it to Washington at 6 A.M., in time for the 9 A.M. caucus vote.[12]

Behind closed doors, Hoyer gave a speech quoting Adlai Stevenson and Robert F. Kennedy, soaring rhetoric that brought applause. Ever the nuts-and-bolts, detail-oriented legislator, Pelosi opted to let Murtha give her nominating speech.

When the votes were counted, Pelosi had won 118–95 (two Democrats didn't vote for either). It was a sweet victory for Pelosi. She had attained the powerful job that had eluded her mentor, Phil Burton. She had become the first woman to hold the whip's job in either party. Yet there was a tinge of bitter sweetness to the victory. Her goal of gaining a Democratic majority was still ahead.

NOTES

1. Rep. George Miller, interview with author, Washington, D.C., December 12, 2007.

2. Rebecca Carr, "McKinney Move Disappoints Lewis; Her Apparent Support for Fellow Georgian's Rival Was Due to a Mix-up, She Says, and May Change," *Atlanta Journal Constitution*, August 14, 1999, p. 4A.

3. Greg Lucas, "Legislative Redistricting Could Hurt Condit, Tauscher, Each Would Gain Large Numbers of More Liberal Voters," *San Francisco Chronicle*, September 1, 2001, p. A3.

4. Juliet Eilperin, "The Making of Madam Whip: Fear and Loathing—and Horse Trading—in the Race for the House's No. 2 Democrat," *Washington Post Magazine*, January 6, 2002, p. W27.

5. Elaine S. Povich, "Democrats Eyeing Golden Prize/California Elections Key to Party's Quest to Retake Congress," *Newsday*, October 15, 2000, p. A35.

6. Emelyn Rodriguez, "Pelosi Poised to Pluck a Political Plum," *California Journal*, June 1, 2000.

7. Rep. George Miller, interview with author, Washington, D.C., December 12, 2007.

8. Rutgers, the State University of New Jersey, Thomas Eagleton Institute of Politics, available online at http://www.eagleton.rutgers.edu/e-gov/e-political archive-2000.htm.

9. Juliet Eilperin, "The Making of Madam Whip: Fear and Loathing—and Horse Trading—in the Race for the House's No. 2 Democrat," *Washington Post Magazine*, January 6, 2002, p. W27.

10. San Gejdensen, interview with author, Branford, Connecticut, December 3, 2007.

11. Rep. Steny Hoyer, interview with author, October 24, 2007.

12. Juliet Eilperin, "The Making of Madam Whip: Fear and Loathing—and Horse Trading—in the Race for the House's No. 2 Democrat," *Washington Post Magazine*, January 6, 2002, p. W27.

Chapter 13

MINORITY LEADER

Nancy Pelosi's race for minority whip had taken three years. The race for the next step up on the ladder—minority leader—would be over in 36 hours.

Of course, there were years of prelude that led up to those 36 hours. There would be infighting and angst among Democrats, and disagreement over the course of the country and the direction of the party. All the while, Pelosi refused to be content with the minority whip job.

As House Minority Whip, Nancy Pelosi got a really plum office in the Capitol, right off the House floor, with a lovely view of the Supreme Court across the street. But she refused to hang a lot of pictures or really settle in. The goal, she kept telling everyone, was not to be in the minority for long, so she wouldn't be in that office long. There was work to be done.

That task continued to be daunting. The attacks of September 11, 2001, had rallied the nation around President George W. Bush. Bush decided to invade Afghanistan, where the Al Qaeda terrorists had trained before attacking. Then, he asked Congress for the authority to go to war with Iraq, saying that would further his efforts against terrorism. Republicans in his own party were solidly behind him. But Democrats were split.

Pelosi, from her perch as a member of the Intelligence Committee, had been briefed on all of the spying that had gone on about Iraq and Al Qaeda. She knew as much about the situation as anyone. Others in the Democratic leadership, especially Minority Leader Richard Gephardt of Missouri, had been equally well advised by the Bush administration and the CIA, the spy agency.

They did not agree. In Pelosi's mind, there were two issues. First, there was the issue of whether going to war in Iraq with the intent of toppling the Iraqi leader, Saddam Hussein, was the right thing to do. She didn't think so, particularly since she believed that all diplomatic efforts to get Saddam to ease up on his people and stop looking to build massive weapons had not been exhausted. The other issue was political: If Democrats did not distinguish themselves from Republicans, they would not win votes in November 2002, she believed.

The vote on giving Bush permission to wage war in Iraq was scheduled for October 10, just a month before the November congressional elections. The issue would be fresh in the mind of voters. Pelosi wanted Democrats to stand out.

But some Democratic leaders were wrestling with how to handle a nation at war. They did not want to appear disloyal to the Bush, who was, after all, the commander in chief trying to defend the nation in the aftermath of the September 11, 2001, attacks. They thought that by solidly backing the president on the war and a couple of other national issues and trying to make their case to voters on more local issues, they could pick off seats one by one.

The war vote was a dramatic and emotional one. Debate raged for three days on the House of Representatives floor. It was equally emotional in the Senate.

Pelosi said that going to war in Iraq was the wrong thing to do at that time.

"The clear and present danger that threatens our country is terrorism," she said. "I say flat out that unilateral action against Iraq will be harmful to our war on terrorism."[1]

Richard Gephardt, the minority leader at the time, stuck with Bush.

Gephardt, who had helped draft the resolution, much to the consternation of some Democrats, said that giving Bush the authority to attack Iraq could avert war by demonstrating that the United States is willing to confront Saddam Hussein over his unwillingness to let United Nations inspectors see whether he was trying to build nuclear or biological weapons.

"I believe we have an obligation to protect the United States by preventing him from getting these weapons and either using them himself or passing them or their components on to terrorists who share his destructive intent," said Gephardt.[2]

And in a move that particularly rankled Pelosi, Gephardt said that the vote was not a matter of party loyalty but rather should reflect the conscience of each member. Publicly, Pelosi did not criticize Gephardt, since she was in line to take the job. But other Democrats were not so kind.

Rep. John Conyers, a veteran Michigan Democrat, professed to be "at a loss" as to why Gephardt would side with Bush.[3]

The House vote was 296–133 to authorize the war.

Over in the Senate, the Democrats were equally divided. Minority Leader Tom Daschle of South Dakota favored the resolution, as did Sen. Dianne Feinstein of California. But Barbara Boxer, California's other senator, who was closer to Pelosi ideologically, opposed it. The Senate authorized the war, as well, and Bush sent American troops into Iraq, where they would remain for many years.

Democrats also had divided on other important issues that year. President Bush had proposed a tax cut, which was opposed by some Democrats, but not all. Ten Democrats in the House supported the tax cut, and 12 Democrats in the Senate provided the winning margin in that chamber.

In the campaigns of 2002, House members had no unifying theme to bring them together.[4]

Rep. George Miller, Pelosi's friend and confidant, said it was difficult to unite the Democrats when there were such obvious splits in the party. Many other Democrats felt the same way.[5]

The 2002 congressional elections in November were a disaster for Democrats. They had hoped to cut into the Republicans majority but instead lost six seats, giving the GOP an even bigger majority, 229–205, with one independent.

The next day, Gephardt stepped down as minority leader. But he retained his seat as a representative from Missouri, indicating that he was planning a run for president in 2004.

Pelosi issued a public statement praising Gephardt, but privately many Democrats blamed him for losing elections in 1996, 1998, 2000, and 2002. He just wasn't getting it done, they complained.

Pelosi's statement also was her announcement that she was officially running for leader. She'd really been running for years, of course, but every time she was approached about it, she'd deflect the issue. "People would come up to me and say, 'Count me in.' And I'd say, 'You understand I'm not asking,'" she said at the time. But she certainly was ready when Gephardt officially stepped down.[6]

As soon as she knew that Gephardt would be leaving the job, Pelosi got on the telephone from her office in San Francisco. She had a list of 100 names of Democratic members to call and check off to see if they would support her. Not for nothing had she spent years working for the election of Democratic candidates. Not for nothing had she raised $8 million over the previous decade for Democratic candidates. The work was about to be rewarded.

By the time her chief rival jumped into the race, Pelosi knew she had it won.[7]

But Rep Martin Frost of Texas, a more middle-of-the road Democrat, didn't. Frost, who also had been campaigning and fundraising for members for years, thought he had a shot at the job. He went on television that day to announce he was campaigning for it. Pelosi was still working the phones.

Frost outlined what he thought the decision facing Democrats was. "Our party must make a choice and decide whether we want to speak to the center of the country or whether we want to speak to a narrow segment," he said.[8]

But, despite her liberal leanings, Pelosi had covered her bases. In addition to cultivating "Old Bull" conservative Democrats like John Murtha of Pennsylvania, she had reached out to newer moderates, too. For example, she brought in to her inner circle Rep. Carolyn McCarthy of Long Island, New York, who once had been a Republican. McCarthy had been persuaded by Democratic Party leaders to switch allegiances and run for Congress after her husband was killed and her son severely wounded in the Long Island Rail Road shooting in 1993, when a mentally ill man shot up the train with a pistol, killing six and wounding 19. McCarthy ran against Rep. Dan Frisa, a Republican who had opposed more restrictive gun laws, something she made into a cause after the shootings, and she won. But many of her constituents were Republicans, just as she had once been. She could not afford to be seen as any kind of wide-eyed liberal. Pelosi brought McCarthy into her circle as a deputy whip, and the inclusiveness paid off. McCarthy announced she would be supporting Pelosi because Pelosi pledged to respect their differences while holding the party together.[9]

Frost had his chits, as well. He had headed the Democratic Congressional Campaign Committee, the organization that works to elect Democrats, in 1998, when Democrats unexpectedly gained seats (though not enough for the majority). He was credited with modernizing the DCCC's efforts by recruiting good candidates and teaching them the ropes of campaigning. Frost was then named chairman of the House Democratic Caucus and helped hone the party's message, from 1998 to 2002. He argued that, as a Democrat from an increasingly Republican state, Texas, he knew how to handle the GOP.

But what he hadn't counted on was Pelosi's head start. After a day of attempting to round up votes and finding that so many had already pledged to support Pelosi, he played the pragmatist, dropped out of the race, and endorsed her. It was over almost before it started.

Nonetheless, Pelosi was taking names. A couple of years later, when Frost wanted to head up the Democratic National Committee after the 2004 elections, Pelosi lobbied hard against him. It was another case of her playing hardball politics and saying something like, "You want to run against me, fine, but don't think there won't be consequences." She refused to discuss her opposition, telling an interviewer a couple of years later only that "Anybody who's ever dealt with me knows not to mess with me."[10]

And yet, there was a softer, personal side to the relationship. When Frost's wife, a retired Army major general, died, in 2006, Pelosi interrupted her campaign schedule to attend the funeral at Arlington National Cemetery and walked behind the caisson and riderless horse that carried Kathryn Frost's casket. She then scheduled a meeting with Frost and thanked him for his help for the party. The relationship had been repaired.[11]

"She's tough," Frost said after Pelosi became Speaker. "That's okay, I'm for tough. Democrats need discipline."[12]

It was that discipline that carried Pelosi through the minority leader's race. After Frost dropped out, Rep. Harold Ford of Tennessee briefly jumped in. Ford claimed to be more conservative than Pelosi and also would have become the first African-American to hold the job. But his candidacy was almost symbolic for all the impact it had. Pelosi won with 177 votes to Ford's 29.

She emerged from the closed caucus meeting of Democrats to cheers, wearing a broad smile and a fire-engine red suit that stood out among all the navy blue or grey suits worn by most of the men. Steny Hoyer, Pelosi's old rival for minority whip, had finally gotten that job, having been elected unanimously by the caucus. Rep. Robert Menendez, a Hispanic from New Jersey, got the No. 3 position, chairman of the caucus, and Rep. James Clyburn of South Carolina, an African American, was awarded the fourth-ranking position, vice chairman of the caucus. Pelosi called the resulting tableau of the four of them "a picture of America."

Republicans were somewhat gleeful as well because they thought they could demonize Pelosi as some kind of left-wing "latte liberal" or "San Francisco-style Democrat," which had implications of ties to the gay community. They felt they could use that to their advantage, and in the following years, they would try to do so.

Rep. Tom DeLay of Texas, the Republican's Majority Leader, who would be the first to try to cast Pelosi as a demon, was restrained that day. He called her a "worthy opponent." She appeared to be just that and left no doubt that she was planning to be a tough leader.[13]

"Where we can find our common ground on the economy and on other domestic issues, we shall seek it," Pelosi said on that day. "Where we cannot find that common ground, we must stand our ground."[14]

NOTES

1. Edward Epstein, "Bush Gets Power to Strike Iraq," *San Francisco Chronicle*, October 11, 2002, p. A1.

2. CNN.com, Friday, October 11, 2002, http://archives.cnn.com/2002/ALLPOLITICS/10/11/iraq.us/.

3. Edward Epstein, "Bush Gets Power to Strike Iraq," *San Francisco Chronicle*, October 11, 2002, p. A1.

4. CNN, March 9, 2001, http://archives.cnn.com/2001/ALLPOLITICS/03/09/bush.budget/index.html.

5. Edward Epstein, "Gephardt Quits House Role," *San Francisco Chronicle*, November 7, 2002, p. A7.

6. Marc Sandalow, "Politics: Democratic Party; Savvy, Cash clinched Job for Pelosi; Tightly Orchestrated Campaign Followed Lucrative Fund Raising," *San Francisco Chronicle*, November 17, 2002, p. 1A.

7. Ibid.

8. Elaine S. Povich, "Democrats Consider New Leader, Direction," *Newsday*, November 8, 2002, p. A5.

9. Ibid.

10. Karen Tumulty and Perry Bacon Jr., "Did Nancy Pelosi Get the Message?" *Time Magazine*, November 19, 2006.

11. Ibid.

12. Martin Frost, interview with author, Washington, D.C., December11, 2006.

13. Marc Sandalow, "History-Making Vote for S.F.'s Pelosi;1st Woman Chosen House Minority Leader," *San Francisco Chronicle*, November 15, 2002, p. A1.

14. Ibid.

Chapter 14

BREAKING THE MARBLE CEILING

Nancy Pelosi got her shoe back—Cinderella style.

In 2006, a wayward airplane drifted into the air space above the Capitol, which had been off limits to aircraft since the 2001 terrorist attacks on New York and Washington. The Capitol was evacuated, and thousands of members of Congress, senators, staff members, and tourists streamed out of the doors and down the steps to the Capitol grounds. Police officers urged them to hurry to staging areas across the street from the Capitol.

It was chaos. The plane was later determined to have been harmless, and everyone went back to work, including Pelosi. But in the melee, she had lost a shoe.

Some days later, Rep. Dave Reichert, a Republican from Washington State, called a press conference to report that he had found the wayward footwear. To applause, he dropped to his knees, Prince Charming style, and fitted the delicate shoe back on Pelosi's foot.

"There's one advantage that men have here: they have shoes tied to their feet," Pelosi quipped.[1]

Pelosi was joking, but throughout her career, there had been other advantages that men have had, and the first one may be that no one ever called a press conference to declare that he had found a man's shoe.

Pelosi's political history in some ways parallels the women's movement in the 1960s and 1970s. In the 1960s, women were just coming around to recognizing the injustice in the fact that they were still treated unequally with men. Women could not get credit cards in their own names if they were married, and there was no such thing as "equal pay for equal work" laws. Classified ads in newspapers were segregated into "help wanted, men" and "help wanted, women" sections. The landmark Supreme Court decision Roe v. Wade, which legalized abortion across the country, would not come until 1973.

As she was raising her children in the 1960s, she was doing the traditional stay-at-home-mom things, and her political world was volunteering. But as she branched out into more intense political work, so the women's rights movement intensified and grew. In 1964, discrimination in the workplace was outlawed, and in 1972, Title IX of the Civil Rights Act ensured that girls would not be discriminated against in education, even if they went to coed high schools or colleges.

Navigating the world of politics as a woman for Pelosi was a natural outgrowth of her life. She had only brothers growing up and learned to hold her own. She went to an all-women's college and learned that women can hold any position in an academic setting. And she learned the balancing act of a mother of five.

Pelosi didn't get to be Speaker because she was a woman. She became Speaker. And she was a woman. Prior to that time, many female candidates for high office ran as the "woman candidate," such as Rep. Patricia Schroeder of Colorado, who ran for president in 1988 as that kind of candidate. Rep. Geraldine Ferraro of New York, who ran unsuccessfully for vice president in 1984 with the Democrat Walter Mondale, was chosen specifically because she was a woman, in an effort to pump up Mondale's weak candidacy.

Not until Hillary Clinton ran for the Democratic nomination for president in 2007 was there a presidential candidate who ran not as a woman but as a candidate who happened to be female. Pelosi's standing was the same, and she came first.

"I didn't run as a feminist statement," she said. "I didn't run as a woman or say vote for me as a woman. I was surprised at all the attention it got."[2]

She shouldn't have been surprised. Of course it got attention, and that attention came through in many ways—not just the shoe incident, for example, but in other situations, as well.

In 2001, she was asked what it was like to attend White House meetings as House minority whip, and she invoked feminist leaders of the past in her answer, acknowledging those pioneers who had come before her.

"For an instant, I felt as though Susan B. Anthony, Lucretia Mott, Elizabeth Cady Stanton—everyone who'd fought for women's right to vote and for the empowerment of women in politics, in their professions, and in their lives—were there with me in the room. Those women were the ones who had done the heavy lifting, and it was as if they were saying, At last we have a seat at the table."[3]

And at a memorial service for the feminist activist Molly Yard, Pelosi invoked her name as well in remembering the encouragement she had given to Pelosi in terms of running for office.

"You have to know that when women said they were going to do something, they were going to run for office, they were going to try for this, people would always tell them about the obstacles, but not Molly," Pelosi said. "She would say, 'Go for it, let's do it, let's get out there together.'"[4]

The interesting part of Pelosi's career is that she didn't start out as anything like a feminist. The stay-at-home-mom image is not one that invokes rallying cries of "Equal Pay for Equal Work," or anything of the sort.

But her feminism was rooted in the old-fashioned values of hard work and sacrifice. She put her family first.

In the article for *Trinity Magazine*, she advised young women to do the same.

"My advice to young women who are thinking about a commitment to public service: 'Have a life first.' Don't make public service your whole life, first. Don't give in to being totally consumed by it, because you can be.

"Have a family. Nurture your family and if you are single, develop friendships and relationships. Make sure your life in public service is not a total sacrifice of your whole life. Devote time to having a balanced life. Because the success of politics can overwhelm you. You cannot have your personal well-being depend on your political success. This is hard. There will be disappointments and you can't tie everything to it. You must have a sense of self beyond the politics."[5]

Pelosi's sense of self was partially grounded in her relationship with her husband, Paul Pelosi. Paul was raised in San Francisco, and when he brought his own family back there, he made a fortune in business, the stock market, and real estate. Neither of them had planned on Nancy entering politics as an officeholder; she was always behind the scenes. But, as Nancy put it, "I say this hoping that many women in America are listening. Just be ready for the opportunity when it comes."

She seized the opportunity, she said, and her husband was completely supportive, if not thrilled. "He's a lovely man, he loves his sports. He's a guy. And as I said, if I stopped doing this tomorrow, he'd probably be happy. On the other hand, he's happy that I enjoy making the fight that I do."[6]

She also had to have a thick skin. Somehow, a woman politician's wardrobe is fair game for writers and broadcasters and other critics. Pelosi's Armani suits brought all kinds of criticism, from newspaper fashion writers to bloggers.

In a famous column, the *Washington Post* fashion writer Robin Givhan wrote that the suits gave Pelosi a "tone of quiet authority: a look suited

to the Speaker." The column noted that the suit "speaks of a specific approach to authority and clout."[7]

Not surprisingly, the column brought a lot of criticism from those who
thought it was silly to explore a woman's wardrobe—there are not very
many explorations of men politicians' wardrobes, by contrast. But those
articles are a fact of life for any woman politician.

Then there was the scrutiny of her diet. A trim woman who rarely ex-
ercised, Pelosi acknowledged a weakness for chocolate (Ghirardelli, made
in San Francisco, is a favorite). That brought the inevitable dissection
of her food intake, another thing that most men politicians rarely face
(with the possible exception of those overweight politicians who went on
much-publicized diets).

"People will be watching her diet—she apparently eats a shocking
amount of chocolate—when all anyone worried about with previous
House speakers was their appetite for pork.

"Her hair, her hemlines, her heels: All are being buzzed about. No one
would have ever thought to ask former Speaker Dennis Hastert what de-
signer he was wearing," wrote the *New York Daily News*.[8]

And ABC News's *Good Morning America* show unabashedly asked,
"What does Pelosi mean for women?" in its show broadcast the day after
she became the third-highest-ranking member of the U.S. government.[9]

And they followed that segment with one ironically titled "The low-
down on the new high heels."

Pelosi concentrated on many issues during her political life, not just
so-called women's issues such as the availability of quality childcare or
equal pay. She argued that national security, the economy, and the environment are women's issues. She would say that lifting the minimum
wage is a women's issue because more women earn low salaries than men.
She would say that changing Medicare, the government program for the
retired elderly, is a women's issue because there are more old women than
old men in the United States.

And, conversely, she would argue that those "women's issues" should be
everyone's issues. "I guess they're called women's issues because if women
did not focus on them, there really wouldn't be any chance of [getting
something done]," she said.[10]

And yet she was not unaware of the impact her position had on other
women. If there was ever any doubt, it was erased when 500 women showed
up at a church service before her installation as speaker in 2007 wearing
"Rosie the Riveter" T-shirts with Pelosi's picture superimposed on the
face, wearing pearl earrings, with the inscription "A woman's place is in
the House—as Speaker." Even the service oozed feminism. She chose the

white lilies for the altar, because they were her favorite flower. The chapel was Trinity University's—still an all-women's college.

She was surrounded by her grandchildren, one of whom shrieked loudly and had to be walked around by his mother, Pelosi's daughter Alexandra. And she held an afternoon tea after the religious service, something no incoming speaker had ever done in the 217 years of the nation's history.

"We've waited over 200 years for this time," Pelosi said at the tea. "America's working women, women working at home, whatever they choose to do, they have a friend in the Capitol of the United States."[11]

There were 22 women in the House when Pelosi was first elected in 1987. When she took over as speaker, there were a record 71. Women were moving into chairmanships of committees and other leadership posts in the Congress. But many of them, Pelosi included, wanted to be considered as leaders first and women second.

"I have always asked my colleagues to judge me by the quality of my leadership and the results we achieve together, not as the first woman," Pelosi said.

But, she added: "Becoming the first woman speaker will send a message to young girls and women across the country that anything is possible for them, that women can achieve power, wield power and breathe the air at that altitude. As the first woman speaker of the House, I will work to make certain that I will not be the last."[12]

NOTES

1. Susan McGinnis, CBS Morning News, May 15, 2005.

2. Peggy Lewis, "Profile: Nancy Pelosi '62: House Democratic Leader," *Trinity College Magazine*, 2002. Available at www.trinitydc.edu/admissions/magazine_profile_pelosi.php.

3. Nancy Pelosi, speech given to the American Association of University Women, June 25, 2005. Available at www.house.gov/pelosi/press/releases/june05/AAUW.html.

4. Nancy Pelosi, memorial service for Molly Yard, November 17, 2005, Office of Nancy Pelosi.

5. Peggy Lewis, "Profile: Nancy Pelosi '62: House Democratic Leader," *Trinity College Magazine*, 2002. Available at www.trinitydc.edu/admissions/profiles/magazine.profile_pelosi.php.

6. Tavis Smiley, interview with Pelosi transcript, October 22, 2007. Available at http://www.pbs.org/kcet/tavissmiley/archive/200710/20071022.html.

7. Robin Givhan, "Muted Tones of Quiet Authority: A Look Suited to the Speaker," *Washington Post*, November 10, 2006, p. C1

8. Helen Kennedy, "Pelosi Coverage Isn't All Politics: Speaker's Style, Diet Scrutinized," *New York Daily News*, January 6, 2007, p. 3A.

9. Diane Sawyer and Robin Roberts, "Madam Speaker, What Does Pelosi Mean for Women?" *Good Morning America,* ABC News, January 5, 2007.

10. Marie Cocco, "This Is What a Speaker Looks Like," *Ms. Magazine,* Winter 2007, pp. 34–37.

11. Faye Fiore and Tina Daunt, "Pelosi Shows She's the Head of Her Party," *Los Angeles Times,* January 4, 2007, p. 1.

12. The Democratic Daily, January 3, 2007. Available at http://thedemocratic daily.com.

Chapter 15

THE IRAQ WAR

On May Day, 2003, President George W. Bush flew in a S-3B Viking aircraft onto an aircraft carrier, clambered out of the plane wearing a jumpsuit and helmet, and declared "mission accomplished" in the Iraq War.

But the war was not over.

The war went on for years. And the American public began to turn away from the president and toward those, like Nancy Pelosi, who opposed the combat from the beginning.

At the end of 2003, 64 percent of the American public, as measured by public opinion polls, said that going to war against Iraq was the right thing to do. But a year later, only 46 percent thought so. By May 2006, support was down to 39 percent. And in November 2006, around Election Day, support remained just as low.[1]

In the beginning of the war, Pelosi was muted in her opposition. On the day war was declared on Iraq by the president, she said simply that Americans "stand behind our men and women in uniform."[2]

People in the country were expecting a short war, and at first they thought they had gotten one. When the president landed on the aircraft carrier to make his pronouncement, only 138 soldiers had died in Iraq. But things began to deteriorate from there. A year later, the death toll in the war was up to 734, with 596 having died since the president declared that major combat operations in Iraq had ended.[3] Many more would die before American troops began to pull out of Iraq.

In the middle of 2003, restive Democrats, including Pelosi, began to sense that all was not going well for the war, despite Bush's proclamations. Pelosi and other senior Democrats called on Bush to "secure the peace" in Iraq. Their letter indicated that they were concerned about the rise of terrorism from the ashes of the Iraq war.[4] But their criticism continued to be muted.

Later that year, Pelosi criticized Bush for a speech at the United Nations in which the United States seemed to be going it alone in the Iraq war. While there were some troops from other nations involved in the fighting, most of the soldiers were American. Pelosi noted that the costs for the war were mounting and that priorities at home were being neglected.[5]

Then, one day in the middle of December 2003, came the most welcome news to Americans since the fall of Baghdad. The Iraqi leader Saddam Hussein, the "Butcher of Baghdad," had been captured. It was an ignominious end to the once-powerful leader. He was found hiding in an underground bunker, unshaven, alone, and apparently disoriented. The American troops captured him alive and knew that he would stand trial for murdering his own people over the years, some with chemical weapons.

Pelosi called the capture "great news" but added a caveat. "As the mission continues, I hope we will see an increased willingness to cooperate by Iraqis previously reluctant to assist the efforts to rid the country of Saddam Hussein's allies."[6]

But the war news was not always good. Amid mounting U.S. casualties, news came out in April 2004 that Americans had abused Iraqi prisoners at Abu Ghraib prison, near Baghdad. The ensuing outcry put American troops in a bad light and added to the mounting distaste for the war.

Pelosi, not wanting to undermine the confidence of U.S. troops in combat, said that the Abu Ghraib incident was disgraceful and damaging to the United States and also to the bulk of the troops, who were performing admirably in the war.

Yet she could not help but realize that the revelations of the atrocities at the prison had helped continue to turn the tide of public opinion further away from support of the Iraq war policy. She asked many questions and called for a full investigation.[7]

As the war reached into its second year, Pelosi's criticism mounted in the face of evidence that the reasons President Bush gave for going to war in the first place—that Saddam Hussein had weapons of mass destruction—turned out to be false.

"The President now says that the war is really about the spread of democracy in the Middle East," Pelosi said at the time. "This effort at after-the-fact justification was only made necessary because the primary rationale was so sadly lacking in fact."[8]

But while public sentiment was turning against the war, there were still many who supported it, and that difference of opinion in the nation was reflected in the Congress. Even among Democrats, there was a diversity of opinion on the war. Some wanted an immediate pullout of American troops, some thought there should be a timetable for withdrawal, and others thought it was foolhardy to put a time constraint on fighting a war. Still others believed that fighting in Iraq was a mission that could not be abandoned.

Pelosi was attempting, as minority leader, to do two things at once when it came to the war. She wanted to hold Democrats together as much as possible, and she also was looking to win back the majority in the House in the 2006 elections.

But the end of 2005, Pelosi's public stance was that while Democrats would produce an issue agenda for the 2006 elections, but it would not take a formal stance on Iraq. Pelosi, herself, at endorsed the proposal by Rep. John Murtha, conservative Pennsylvania Democrat, who had called for a swift redeployment of American forces from Iraq over a period of six months, but no other party leaders took that position, and House Minority Whip Steny Hoyer, the Maryland Democrat, publicly opposed her.[9]

On the other end of the spectrum, back at home in San Francisco, Pelosi was hearing from a vocal group of people who wanted Pelosi to come out strongly for removing all American troops from Iraq immediately. While in Washington she was seen as a peacenik, in San Francisco she was seen as a "warmonger." She was forced to explain to the radical left-wing protestors who heckled her at every turn that while she thought the war in Iraq was a "grotesque mistake in my view—a tragedy," she did not want to immediately cut off funding for those troops already in Iraq. She was trying to walk something of a middle ground, making neither side in the war debate happy.[10]

The drumbeat against the war got louder and stronger as the year went on and the elections of 2006 heated up. Pelosi was traveling all across the country campaigning for Democrats in one massive push to finally win a majority in the House. Everywhere she went, it seemed, sentiment against the war was growing. That feeling was bolstered by the fact that many of the soldiers fighting in the war had their tours of duty extended two and three times. People felt that was unfair, and they were missing their soldiers—particularly those who had signed up for the National Guard, a branch of the service that was designed to guard the homeland and to fight a real war only under extraordinary circumstances.

In June 2006, some 2,500 troops had been killed in the Iraq war and 18,000 wounded and the cost had risen to $400 billion. And the news out of Iraq continued to be bad. The fledgling Iraqi government was having trouble holding the country together. Insurgents were blowing up cars and open-air markets seemingly at will. Some social progress was being made in Iraq, with new schools and other government buildings being con-structed, but somehow that seemed small in comparison to the mayhem.

That month, the House engaged in some of the most passionate and pointed debate about the Iraq war since its beginning 39 months before. Ostensibly, the debate was over a nonbinding resolution, just an expres-sion of sentiment, to honor the troops and to praise the resolve of the Iraqi people while maintaining that the U.S. would eventually prevail in Iraq. But, in reality, it focused the political debate over the war—which had been going on across the country for more than a year—directly on the floor of the House of Representatives.

Republicans, including House Speaker Dennis Hastert of Illinois, took the highly unusual step of opening the debate. Most times, the Speaker of the House does not participate in debates. When Speakers do par-ticipate, they usually speak at the end of the discussion, not the begin-ning. Hastert crystallized the political discussion calling for the nation to stand "firm in our commitment to fight terrorism and the evil it inflicts throughout the world."[11]

Pelosi simply said that the war in Iraq is a "failed policy" and voted against the resolution. "Everything the Republicans have told us, every-thing the president and the administration have said, have been wrong," she said.[12]

As summer turned into fall, the war began to play a bigger and bigger role in the elections. Pelosi warned that a Republican victory would pro-long the fighting another 10 years, while President Bush and the Repub-licans insisted that a win by Democrats would leave the troops stranded in hostile territory.[13]

"This election is about Iraq," Pelosi said. She was about to find out just how much.

NOTES

1. New York Times-CBS News poll, 12/10-13/03 to 7/20-22/07. Available at http://www.nytimes.com/ref/us/polls_index.html.

2. Office of Nancy Pelosi, statement, March 19, 2003.

3. David Paul Kuhn, "'Mission Accomplished' Revisited," April 30, 2004, available at www.cbsnews.com/stories/2004/04/30/politics/main614998.shtml.

4. Office of Nancy Pelosi, Press Release, July 28, 2003.

5. Office of Nancy Pelosi, Press Release, September 23, 2003.

6. Office of Nancy Pelosi, Press Release, December 14, 2003.

7. Office of Nancy Pelosi, Press Release, May 4, 2004.

8. Office of Nancy Pelosi, statement, March 16, 2005.

9. Dan Balz, "Pelosi Hails Democrats' Diverse War Stances," *Washington Post*, December 16, 2005, p. A23.

10. Erin McCormick, "Anti-war Activists Take Pelosi to Task; Minority Leader Negotiates with Lawmakers on Her Right," *San Francisco Chronicle*, January 15, 2006, p. B1.

11. Edward Epstein, "House War Debate Stirs Partisan Fervor," *San Francisco Chronicle*, June 16, 2006.

12. Ibid.

13. Marc Sandalow, "Pelosi's Countdown: She Ticks Off a List of Changes, Including a New Iraq Strategy," *San Francisco Chronicle*, November 5, 2006, p. A1.

Chapter 16

SPEAKER OF THE HOUSE

When the telephone rang early in the morning Wednesday, November 9, 2006, Pelosi figured it had to be news from her daughter, Alexandra, who was expecting Pelosi's sixth grandchild. Who else would be calling at the crack of dawn?

The president of the United States, that's who.

President George W. Bush was calling to congratulate Pelosi on the election victories the night before, which would make her Speaker of the House.

She picked up the phone and said: "Do we have a baby coming?"

"Leader Pelosi?" inquired the startled White House operator.

Assured that it was the minority leader and soon-to-be Speaker, President Bush got on the line to offer congratulations on becoming the first woman Speaker of the House, no matter that his own party was trounced in the elections, due in no small measure to Pelosi's tireless work against him and his Republicans.[1]

In so many ways, this was Pelosi's election and Pelosi's victory.

Almost a year earlier, a reporter had asked Pelosi whether her position against the war might hurt her chances to return as minority leader of the House.

"I fully intend to be standing here as Speaker of the House next year. Any other questions?" Pelosi snapped.[2]

The Republicans had tried throughout the year to make the election about her. They labeled her a "San Francisco-style" Democrat, a thinly veiled reference to the liberalism and to the gay community in her city. They ran advertisements with a scary image of her face superimposed on the faces of Democratic candidates around the country in an effort to demonize her. It was a different kind of attack from the ones years earlier in which she was scorned as a lightweight and a dilettante. Now, they were aware of her power and were trying to scare people into believing that she would be too radical to lead the Congress.

But she had friends. She had raised more than $50 million for Democrats over the years, and they were indebted to her. Her opposition to the war in Iraq was steadfast and consistent, in contrast to that of many in Congress who had once supported the war but then became skeptical.

She had a plan, hatched in the ashes of the 2004 election when Democrats lost three seats in the House instead of picking up seats as they had hoped. The plan was to find more moderate and conservative Democrats and persuade them to run for the House. She also refused to compromise on Social Security and other issues important to Democrats, in an effort to draw clear distinctions with Bush and the Republicans. Pelosi and Rahm Emanuel, the take-no-prisoners congressman from Illinois whom she appointed to head the Democratic Congressional Campaign Committee, worked the situation continuously to get Democrats elected to Congress.

For example, in Indiana, they recruited sheriff Brad Ellsworth to run against the Republican incumbent, John Hostettler, a three-term member of the House. Republicans tried to tie Ellsworth to Pelosi, saying he would be a vote for her kind of liberalism. It didn't work, and the conservative Ellsworth defeated Hostettler.[3]

As she dashed around the country working for Democratic victories, she got better and better at it. She combined her inherent gentility with a tough antiwar, anti-Bush message along with proficient money-raising. "Are you ready for a Democratic victory?" she would ask at every stop. Inevitably, the answer was yes.

But it was in the behind-the-scenes strategizing that Pelosi really made her mark. Just as she had done decades earlier in organizing San Francisco for her first race for Congress, she organized the country for Democrats.

She carried an enormous binder with notes on every important congressional race. It wasn't exactly the "favor file" of those long-ago Baltimore years, but the roots of that file were there. It wasn't exactly the list of 30,000 donors she kept in a database at Democratic headquarters, but the fruits of that file were there.

She called candidates in more than five dozen races regularly to check in and to see if they needed more money or strategy tips.[4]

From Atlanta to Pennsylvania and back to her native California, Pelosi crisscrossed the nation, predicting victory but leaving nothing to chance.

Several days before the election, she predicted at least a 15-seat pickup, the number the Democrats needed to take power, if not 22 to 26 more Democratic seats.[5]

On election night, she huddled at the Hyatt Hotel on Capitol Hill in Washington, D.C., with her advisers and Sen. Charles Schumer, the New York Democrat who headed the committee in charge of electing Democrats to the Senate. Also present were Senate Democratic leader Harry Reid of Nevada and Rep. Rahm Emanuel, the Chicago Democrat whom she had tapped to help her win the House. A raucous party was going on in the ballroom. Various politicians were tipping drinks at the lobby bar. Televisions were turned to news channels where reports of Democratic progress were starting to trickle in. Journalists stood poised to record the history-making event.

At about 10 P.M. Eastern time, it was clear—a Democratic victory!

In the ballroom, the crowd exploded. They chanted, "Madam Speaker! Madam Speaker!"

Finally, Pelosi, Schumer, Reid, and Emanuel appeared on the stage, hands raised in victory. "This sounds like a crowd that is ready for victory!" she shouted. But then she spoke in a calm voice that belied her excitement.

"The campaign is over—Democrats are ready to lead," she said. "Today we have made history—now let us make process."

It was very late that night before she went to bed, only to be awakened by the White House call. It was a few days later when her sixth grandchild was actually born, and she and her husband, Paul, jumped on a plane to New York. They admired little Paul Michael Vos (named for his grandfather), dispensed some motherly advice to Alexandra and her husband, Michiel, then flew back to Washington to prepare for her precedent-setting adventure as Speaker.

Pelosi had already staked out a legislative program. She called it the "100 hours" plan, and it set out some of the most important priorities for her speakership.

She pledged to implement the recommendations of the so-called 9/11 Commission on America's security, to increase the minimum wage, to cut interest rates on college loans, to pass new ethics legislation governing House rules, and to allow medical research using embryonic stem cells—something scientists say could hold the link to curing many diseases but that opponents argue destroys human life with the embryos.

While her legislative goals were supported by most Democrats in the House, the party was split by Pelosi's decision to back her old friend and military veteran Rep. John Murtha for majority leader over her old rival, Minority Whip Steny Hoyer, who was next in line for the job. Pelosi felt indebted to Murtha, who had nominated her for Speaker and who had first proposed withdrawing troops from Iraq, which became the party's position and which had, arguably, won it the election. Some Democrats were distressed at the contest, which they said blunted the celebratory spirit they felt after their great election victory.

Nevertheless, Pelosi stuck with Murtha, only to see her choice rejected by the Democratic caucus in a decisive vote on November 16, 149-86. Pelosi and Hoyer pledged to work together, but there were some bruised feelings among the Democrats. Some of them felt that Pelosi should not have destroyed the moment of Democratic victory with the contest, but Pelosi once again showed that loyalty was paramount with her.

Hoyer said that Pelosi always made it clear that there are "consequences for opposing her. People need to know that if you are a leader and you ask people to do things, and they cross you or make things more difficult, if there are no consequences, your effectiveness as a leaders is diminished. She understood that very well."[6]

The Democrats also chose Rep. James Clyburn, an African American from South Carolina, as majority whip and Rep. Rahm Emanuel of Illinois as chairman of the party caucus. There was some speculation initially that Emanuel might challenge Clyburn for the whip's job, putting Pelosi in an awkward position. But Emanuel decided to go for caucus chairman instead when Pelosi promised him greater responsibilities, averting that fight.

In addition to the housekeeping, Pelosi was preparing for her formal ascension as Speaker of the House. The symbolism of her rise to power was almost as important as the legislative program. Pelosi was determined that her installation as Speaker would reflect all that it took to bring her to the historic day.

She combined all the aspects of her life in a four-day celebration surrounding her swearing-in.

First, there was Little Italy. She traveled the 40 miles up the road to Baltimore, the same route she had traveled so many years before, in the opposite direction, to go to Trinity College. This time, she was coming back a heroine. They even named a street after her: "Via Nancy D'Alesandro Pelosi"—the 200 block of Albemarle Street in front of the house where she grew up.

The whole city, especially the "Little Italy" section, turned out to welcome home "Little Nancy," who had brought so much pride to Baltimore.

"I wanted to come back here to say thank you to all of you, for the spirit of community that has always strengthened and inspired my life," Pelosi said, speaking from a makeshift stage put up in front of 245 Albemarle

Street, her childhood home. "Every step that I took to the speakership began in this neighborhood."[7]

She laid a bouquet of white roses at a statue of her father. She went to church at old St. Leo's, the center of her young life in Little Italy. And she went to dinner with her family.

Pelosi also attended Mass at Trinity University, and she put on a tea for several hundred women who wore those "Rosie the Riveter" buttons with Pelosi's face, wearing pearl earrings, superimposed on them. Then, she attended a party at the Italian Embassy in Washington, where the crooner Tony Bennett performed just for her.

The next day, January 4, 2007, was like no other for Pelosi. After another church service in the morning, Pelosi and her family, and hundreds of supporters from San Francisco, traveled to the Capitol. At precisely noon, the hour set by the U.S. Constitution, the House of Representatives was gaveled into session by Karen L. Haas, the clerk. The buzz of excitement was visible even to those in the gallery seats far above the cavernous chamber. As usual, many members had brought their children and grandchildren onto the floor to witness their swearing-in as members of the House. But this year, they would get to witness history, as well.

Rahm Emanuel, who had shared the victory, rose to nominate Pelosi. "As a father of three young children, I am particularly thrilled to be a part of this moment," he said. "Thrilled that a generation of young girls and boys across America are about to witness another historic step in our nation's march toward equality of opportunity." He then put Pelosi's name in nomination for Speaker.

Adam Putnam, another fresh-faced young representative, and a Republican from Florida, rose to nominate John Boehner of Ohio as the Republican's candidate. Putnam called Boehner a man who represents the "best of honesty, integrity, decency, uncanny wisdom and understanding." All that may have been true, but everyone in the chamber knew that since Democrats were in the majority and they would all vote for Pelosi, Boehner was doomed to finish second.

Nonetheless, the time-honored tradition of the voting began. Normally, votes in the 435-member House are recorded on electronic boards that light up to show how a member voted. Each member votes by slipping a voting card the size and shape of a credit card into a slot on the back of some of the chairs in the chamber. But in the ceremonial vote for speaker, each candidate's name is called aloud and each representative responds with the name of the candidate for Speaker. "Pelosi!" "Pelosi!" "Boehner!" "Boehner!" (pronounced bay'-ner) rang out across the chamber.

Some members couldn't resist noting the historic occasion before casting their votes. First-term Rep. Jerry McNerney of California, who defeated the incumbent Republican Richard Pombo with a lot of help from
Pelosi, rose and said, "It is my pleasure to cast my first vote in this House
for Nancy Pelosi."[8]

Even some of her old rivals took note of the moment. Steny Hoyer
noted that he was "happy to cast my vote for Maryland's favorite daughter." Rep. John Lewis, the Georgia Democrat and civil rights pioneer who
once had envisioned himself standing in Pelosi's place, noted the mo-
mentous occasion: "On this historic day when the eyes of the nation are
upon us and on our history, I am very proud to cast my vote for the young
lady from California, Nancy Pelosi."[9]

Rep. Loretta Sanchez, Democrat of California, said she voted "for the
empowerment of all women in the world." The tally of women in the
House that day was a record-breaking 71.[10]

"Women can do anything!" declared Rep. Nita Lowey, a New York
Democrat, casting her vote for Pelosi. When Lowey came to the House
in 1988, she was one of only 20 women there.

While many of the Republicans in the chamber looked glum—outgoing
Speaker Dennis Hastert of Illinois stood against the rail at the back of the
chamber barely clapping when Pelosi's name was announced—Boehner
rose to the occasion. "Today marks an occasion I think the Founding Fathers would approve of," Boehner said. "Today, whether you are a Democrat, Republican, or independent, today is a cause for celebration."

After about two hours of one-by-one voting, Haas made the announcement: The vote was 233 for Pelosi to 202 for Boehner. Pelosi had been
elected Speaker.

The members of the House rose with cheers. Even Republicans clapped,
some reluctantly. A special "escort committee" was appointed to formally
bring Pelosi back into the chamber, entering from the back, to sustained
applause, handshakes, hugs, and kisses from the members lining the center aisle. It looked for all the world like a State of the Union address, when
the President of the United States enters the chamber with all the clapping and cheers usually reserved for that occasion.

But it was Pelosi, attired in a fitted plum suit and stunning, oversized
pearls, who mounted the podium and took the gavel from Boehner at
2:08 P.M. She held it high, then took a second look at it, as if to make sure
it was real.

"This is an historic moment," Pelosi said in her first remarks as speaker
of the 110th Congress. "It's an historic moment for the Congress. It's an
historic moment for the women of America. It is a moment for which we
have waited for over 200 years."

The election of Pelosi as Speaker was the culmination of what she called the shattering of the "marble ceiling" that had stopped women from holding Congress's highest office since the chamber was first organized, in 1789. During her speech, she looked to her husband, Paul, in the gallery, along with her children and other family members, and thanked them for giving her "the confidence to go from the kitchen to the Congress."

As Pelosi ticked off her plans for the new Congress, one item stood out: Iraq.

"The American people rejected an open-ended obligation to a war without end," she said, bringing Democrats to their feet. "It is the responsibility of the president to articulate a new plan for Iraq that makes it clear to the Iraqis that they must defend their own streets and their own security," she said, "a plan that promotes stability in the region and a plan that allows us to responsibly redeploy our troops."

> In order to achieve our new America for the 21st century, we must return this House to the American people. So our first order of business is passing the toughest congressional ethics reform in history. This new Congress doesn't have 2 years or 200 days. Let us join together in the first 100 hours to make this Congress the most honest and open Congress in history. 100 hours.
>
> This openness requires respect for every voice in the Congress. As Thomas Jefferson said, "Every difference of opinion is not a difference of principle." My colleagues elected me to be Speaker of the House, the entire House. Respectful of the vision of our Founders, the expectation of our people, and the great challenges that we face, we have an obligation to reach beyond partisanship to work for all Americans.
>
> Let us stand together to move our country forward, seeking common ground for the common good. We have made history; now let us make progress for the American people.[11]

As she finished her speech, she invited her grandchildren up to the podium with her and then extended the invitation to include all the children and grandchildren of the members of the House, who eagerly climbed up to the podium. Pelosi held the gavel high. Some of the kids looked at it in awe. Others stared out into the vast chamber, looking for their relatives, and wondering, perhaps, if they might someday be the one getting the cheers.

Pelosi banged the huge gavel against the large wooden block with authority. "For these children, for all America's children, the house will come to order," Pelosi said, the authoritative sound of her voice and the banging of the gavel rising over the din.

It was her House now.

NOTES

1. Nancy Zuckerbrod, "Leader Pelosi Primed for Power: But 'Everything Stops' for Baby," *Chicago Sun-Times*, November 9, 2006. Available at http://www.suntimes.com/news/politics/obama/130378,cst-nws-pelosi09.article.

2. Marc Sandalow, "The Rise of Nancy Pelosi," *San Francisco Chronicle*, November 10, 2006, p. A1.

3. Jim VandeHei and Chris Cillizza, "Groundhog Day, New Day, More Conservative Dems," *Washington Post*, September 21, 2006. Available at www.washingtonpost.com.

4. Marc Sandalow, "The Rise of Nancy Pelosi," *San Francisco Chronicle*, November 10, 2006, p. A1.

5. Marc Sandalow, "Pelosi's Countdown: She Ticks Off a List of Changes, Including a New Iraq Strategy," *San Francisco Chronicle*, November 5, 2006, p. A1.

6. Steny Hoyer, interview with author, Washington, D.C., October 24, 2007.

7. Matthew Hay Brown, "All Signs Point to Home: House Speaker Nancy Pelosi Is Honored in Little Italy, Where She Grew Up, with a Street Named after Her," *Baltimore Sun*, January 6, 2007, p. 1B.

8. Edward Epstein and Zachary Coile, "Madam Speaker; Pelosi Picks Up Gavel, She Becomes the Most Powerful Woman in American Politics, Second in the Line of Succession to the Presidency," *San Francisco Chronicle*, January 5, 2007, p. A1.

9. Ibid.

10. John M. Broder and Robin Toner, "The 110th Congress: Jubilant Democrats Assume Control on Capitol Hill," *New York Times*, January 5, 2007.

11. Office of The Speaker of the House, speech at the opening of the 110th Congress, January 4, 2007.

Chapter 17

PELOSI'S POWER

Pelosi's first order of business was to have her House pass a new measure to limit gifts to lawmakers from lobbyists, one bill in a series of efforts to "drain the swamp" that Congress had become in the minds of many voters. That bill passed nearly unanimously, though Republicans complained about the speed with which she acted. But with representatives wanting to try to enhance the image of Congress, there was little resistance to the actual rules changes.

However, Pelosi was to find out that governing in the unruly House, which some have compared to "herding cats," was not always going to be that easy.

To put it in some perspective, the Democrats held a 28-seat majority in the House. That was enough to get much of the Democratic agenda through, but not always. And over in the Senate, Democrats had an even slimmer margin. In addition, the Senate's filibuster rules called for 60 votes to break a filibuster, an endless round of debate. So, effectively, the magic number to pass legislation in the Senate was 60, not 51.

And President Bush stood ready with his veto pen to stymie any other legislation he didn't agree with.

In the next week, Democrats rammed through bills to make good on Pelosi's promises. The bills raised the minimum wage, lifted restrictions on federal financing of embryonic stem cell research, and allowed the government to negotiate price cuts with pharmaceutical companies for the Medicare prescription drug program. The House also passed bills to lower rates on student loans and to roll back subsidies for oil and gas producers.

The bills went to the Senate and were passed there, too. But only four became law: the minimum wage hike, implementation of the 9/11 commission recommendations, college cost reduction, and the energy measure. The stem cell bill was vetoed by Bush.

Pelosi also moved swiftly to ban smoking in the one room where it was still allowed on the House side of the Capitol—the "Speaker's Lobby," just off the House floor. For years, the lobby had been the place where cigarettes, cigars, and pipes burned freely. Even after smoking was banned in most other places in the Capitol, the Speaker's Lobby was a singular refuge for smokers, who included some members of the House, including the former Majority Leader John Boehner. But Boehner and the others were resigned to the fact that they were no longer allowed to relax in leather stuffed armchairs and smoke. The era of the "smoke-filled room" was over.[1]

INTELLIGENCE COMMITTEE CONTROVERSY

While the smoking ban may have ruffled some feathers on Capitol Hill, it was nothing compared to the controversy over who would become chairman of the House Select Committee on Intelligence, where Pelosi had served with such length and distinction. As Speaker, she got to decide who would head the panel. Rep. Jane Harman, the California veteran politician whom Pelosi had persuaded to run again for the House, was in line for the job. From the outside, she seemed perfect—smart, experienced, and judicious. But Pelosi had begun to doubt her loyalty, particularly after Harman, in Pelosi's judgment, was insufficiently critical of President Bush and the Iraq war. In fact, from Pelosi's point of view, Harman seemed to be endorsing some aspects of the war a little too much. Pelosi needed someone in that job who was going to be as critical of the war as she was. She started looking around for alternatives.

The first alternative was no prize. Second in line for the job by seniority was Rep. Alcee Hastings of Florida. Hastings had served with distinction in the House, but before he was elected, he had been impeached and removed from a federal judgeship in 1989 in Florida because of a bribery scandal. He was never convicted of anything, which is why he could run successfully for the House, but that tainted background posed problems for Pelosi because of the sensitive nature of the Intelligence Committee business. However, Hastings was African American, and Pelosi did not want to offend that constituency, making her choice even more difficult.

After Hastings in seniority was Rep. Silvestre Reyes, a Hispanic member from Texas. While the demographics of that choice appealed to Pelosi, he lacked the experience the other two candidates had. He maintained a low profile and tended to relate intelligence activities to his experience as a member of the U.S. Border Patrol in Texas. However, Reyes had opposed the Iraq war from the outset, like Pelosi.

By letting it be known that she was displeased with Harman, Pelosi opened up speculation for weeks as to whom she would name to head the panel. Harman started lobbying for the post, even calling on outside groups, such as the American Israel Public Affairs Committee, to lobby Pelosi. That backfired, because Pelosi did not take well to being pressured from the outside.[2]

She chose Reyes.

Other committees were headed by long-time supporters, too. George Miller, one of her closest confidants, was made chairman of the Education and Labor Committee. Rep. Barney Frank of Massachusetts, one of a handful of openly gay members of Congress, headed the Financial Services panel. Two African Americans, Rep. John Conyers of Michigan and Rep. Charles Rangel of New York, were at the top of the Judiciary and the Ways and Means Committees, respectively. Rep. Nydia Velazquez, a Hispanic woman, chaired the Small Business Committee. While many of these jobs came to the members by seniority, Pelosi had a hand in all of them.

Pelosi did not seek to pass over veteran Rep. John Dingell of Michigan. Dingell still got to head the powerful Energy and Commerce Committee, despite his differences with Pelosi a long time ago. His seniority seemed to trump it all, and he became an ally.

ACCOMPLISHMENTS

Pelosi put the environment and global warming issues near the top of her agenda, as well. She established a special committee to look into global warming and called for all of the committees to pass environmentally friendly legislation.

Congress, after much wrangling all of that first year, finally approved an energy bill to increase mileage standards for cars and trucks by 40 percent by the year 2020. The compromise energy bill package was far narrower than Pelosi had initially hoped, but the accomplishment stood out, nonetheless. Dingell, who had represented Detroit, the home of American car manufacturers, for years, was resistant to the higher mileage standards because they would cost the auto manufacturers more money. She pushed hard, and he pushed back. She won. And, in the end, he signed onto Pelosi's energy bill and praised her efforts.

"Is it a perfect bill?" he asked in a speech on the House floor. "No. But it is good enough to be supported by the members. Its core is a series of requirements that will improve energy efficiency of almost every product and tool and appliance that is used in the United States from light bulbs to light trucks."[3]

Pelosi talked about the bill, as she did so many things, in terms of the future and the children. "It is as global as the planet, and the opportunity provided to take us to a new horizon, to see a new world, a new era of possibility. I hope, as a Christmas to our constituents and, especially to the children, because it's about their future."[4]

Rep. George Miller's take on the energy bill was that Pelosi simply "got it done." It wasn't exactly the way she would have like it to be, but she was pragmatic enough to get what she could and save the rest for another day. "She did not come here to waste time," Miller said. "Results are related to time."[5]

That first Congress with Pelosi in charge also put more money into veterans' needs and passed the most significant gun-control legislation since the early 1990s. Congress also allocated more money for math and science teachers who earn advanced credentials in their field, gave tax relief for homeowners facing loss of their homes, passed bills doubling money for basic research, and made more efforts to help out the Gulf Coast, which had been devastated by Hurricane Katrina, in 2005.

But on her signature issue of the war in Iraq, Pelosi's first year proved a disappointment. She was not able to achieve her goal of cutting off funding for the war or forcing the president to pledge to bring the troops home by a specific date. In the end, both the House and Senate voted to fund the war in 2007, though Democrats in the House voted 141 to 78 against it.

President Bush prevailed over Pelosi on every aspect of the Iraq fight in 2007, beginning with a nonbinding resolution opposing the troop buildup that year and ending with the appropriation of $70 billion in unrestricted war funds by December 2007.[6]

Some Democrats were discouraged. But not Pelosi. She vowed to keep on striving toward the goals she had set for herself. She was throwing herself into the next election cycle, hoping to bolster her majority as she had done before.

She continued to stand as a symbol of equality and power, traveling around the country and the globe, representing herself, her country, and her country's women. And, in 2007, she welcomed her seventh grandchild, Thomas Vincent Vos, brother of the little boy whose arrival she assumed was behind that early-morning call from the president after the election that made her Speaker of the House.

While she had never sought to be a symbol, it was inescapable. In the fall of 2007, a special election in Massachusetts brought a new congresswoman into the House, Niki Tsongas. Tsongas had been around politics for many years—her husband had been a U.S. representative and senator and had run for president in 1992, before he died of cancer, in 1997. But the thrill of being elected to the House herself was still fresh for Tsongas.

When Tsongas stood in the well of the House to be sworn into office, it was Pelosi who stood on the podium to swear her in: one woman, administering the oath of office to another. In a flashback to Pelosi's experience 20 years earlier, Tsongas's first speech was short.

"It has been a real honor and pleasure and treasure to be sworn in by the first female House Speaker," Tsongas said, looking over her shoulder to smile at Pelosi.

Pelosi beamed down at her from the podium, a powerful woman presiding over the United States House of Representatives. The symbolism of the moment was obvious, her ambition unbounded, and her career unfinished.

NOTES

1. Brody Mullins, "In Nancy Pelosi's House, It's No Ifs, Ands or Butts," *Wall Street Journal*, January 11, 2007.

2. Mark Mazzetti, "For a Top Democrat, Further Climb Seems Out," *New York Times*, October 24, 2006.

3. The Congressional Record, December 18, 2007, p. H16740.

4. Ibid., p. H16748.

5. Rep. George Miller, interview with author, Washington, D.C., December 7, 2007.

6. Jonathan Wesisman and Paul Kane, "Key Setbacks Dim Luster of Democrats' Year," *Washington Post*, December 20, 2007, p. A1.

Appendix I

WOMEN IN THE U.S. HOUSE OF REPRESENTATIVES

1917–1929

Name	Party-State	Dates Served
Jeannette Rankin	Rep.-Mont.	1917–1919; 1941–1943
Alice Mary Robertson	Rep.-Okla.	1921–1923
Winnifred Sprague Mason Huck	Rep.-Ill.	1922–1923
Mae Ella Nolan	Rep.-Calif.	1923–1925
Florence Prag Kahn	Rep.-Calif.	1925–1937
Mary Teresa Norton	Dem.-N.J.	1925–1951
Edith Nourse Rogers	Rep.-Mass.	1925–1960
Katherine Gudger Langley	Rep.-Ky.	1927–1931
Pearl Peden Oldfield	Dem.-Ark.	1929–1931
Ruth Hanna McCormick	Rep.-Ill.	1929–1931
Ruth Bryan Owen	Dem.-Fla.	1929–1933
Ruth Sears Baker Pratt	Rep.-N.Y.	1929–1933

1930–1939

Name	Party-State	Dates Served
Effiegene Locke Wingo	Dem.-Ark.	1930–1933
Willa McCord Blake Eslick	Dem.-Tenn.	1932–1933
Kathryn Ellen O'Loughlin (McCarthy)	Dem.-Kan.	1933–1935

Virginia Ellis Jenckes	Dem.-Ind.	1933–1939
Isabella Selmes Greenway	Dem.-Ariz.	1933–1937
Marian Williams Clarke	Rep.-N.Y.	1933–1935
Caroline Love Goodwin O'Day	Dem.-N.Y.	1935–1943
Nan Wood Honeyman	Dem.-Ore.	1937–1939
Elizabeth Hawley Gasque	Dem.-S.C.	1938–1939
Jessie Sumner	Rep.-Ill.	1939–1947
Clara Gooding McMillan	Dem.-S.C.	1939–1941

1940–1949

Name	Party-State	Dates Served
Frances Payne Bolton	Rep.-Ohio	1940–1969
Margaret Chase Smith[1]	Rep.-Maine	1940–1949
Florence Reville Gibbs	Dem.-Ga.	1940–1941
Katharine Edgar Byron	Dem.-Md.	1941–1943
Veronica Grace Boland	Dem.-Pa.	1942–1943
Clare Boothe Luce	Rep.-Conn.	1943–1947
Winifred Claire Stanley	Rep.-N.Y.	1943–1945
Willa Lybrand Fulmer	Dem.-S.C.	1944–1945
Emily Taft Douglas	Dem.-Ill.	1945–1947
Helen Gahagan Douglas	Dem.-Calif.	1945–1951
Chase Going Woodhouse	Dem.-Conn.	1945–1947; 1949–1951
Helen Douglas Mankin	Dem.-Ga.	1946–1947
Eliza Jane Pratt	Dem.-N.C.	1946–1947
Georgia Lee Lusk	Dem.-N.M.	1947–1949
Katharine Price Collier St. George	Rep.-N.Y.	1947–1965
Reva Zilpha Beck Bosone	Dem.-Utah	1949–1953
Cecil Murray Harden	Rep.-Ind.	1949–1959
Edna Flannery Kelly	Dem.-N.Y.	1949–1969

1950–1959

Name	Party-State	Dates Served
Marguerite Stitt Church	Rep.-Ill.	1951–1963
Ruth Thompson	Rep.-Mich.	1951–1957
Maude Elizabeth Kee	Dem.-W.Va.	1951–1965
Vera Daerr Buchanan	Dem.-Pa.	1951–1955
Gracie Bowers Pfost	Dem.-Idaho	1953–1963

Leonor Kretzer Sullivan	Dem.-Mo.	1953–1977
Mary Elizabeth Pruett Farrington[2]	Rep.-Hawaii	1954–1957
Iris Faircloth Blitch	Dem.-Ga.	1955–1963
Edith Starrett Green	Dem.-Ore.	1955–1974
Martha Wright Griffiths	Dem.-Mich.	1955–1974
Coya Gjesdal Knutson	D-Minn.	1955–1959
Kathryn Elizabeth Granahan	Dem.-Pa.	1956–1963
Florence Price Dwyer	Rep.-N.J.	1957–1973
Catherine Dean May	Rep.-Wash.	1959–1971
Edna Oakes Simpson	Rep.-Ill.	1959–1961
Jessica McCullough Weis	Rep.-N.Y.	1959–1963

1960–1969

Name	Party-State	Dates Served
Julia Butler Hansen	Dem.-Wash.	1960–1974
Catherine Dorris Norrell	Dem.-Ark.	1961–1963
Louise Goff Reece	Rep.-Tenn.	1961–1963
Corinne Boyd Riley	Dem.-S.C.	1962–1963
Charlotte Thompson Reid	Rep.-Ill.	1963–1971
Irene Bailey Baker	Rep.-Tenn.	1964–1965
Patsy Takemoto Mink	Dem.-Hawaii	1965–1977; 1990–2002
Lera Millard Thomas	Dem.-Tex.	1966–1967
Margaret M. Heckler	Rep.-Mass.	1967–1983
Shirley Anita Chisholm	Dem.-N.Y.	1969–1983

1970–1979

Name	Party-State	Dates Served
Bella Savitzky Abzug	Dem.-N.Y.	1971–1977
Ella Tambussi Grasso	Dem.-Conn.	1971–1975
Louise Day Hicks	Dem.-Mass.	1971–1973
Elizabeth Bullock Andrews	Dem.-Ala.	1972–1973
Yvonne Brathwaite Burke	Dem.-Calif.	1973–1979
Marjorie Sewell Holt	Rep.-Md.	1973–1987
Elizabeth Holtzman	Dem.-N.Y.	1973–1981
Barbara Charline Jordan	Dem.-Tex.	1973–1979
Patricia Scott Schroeder	Dem.-Colo.	1973–1997

Corinne Claiborne (Lindy) Boggs	Dem.-La.	1973–1991
Cardiss Collins	Dem.-Ill.	1973–1997
Millicent Hammond Fenwick	Rep.-N.J.	1975–1983
Martha Elizabeth Keys	Dem.-Kans.	1975–1979
Marilyn Laird Lloyd	Dem.-Tenn.	1975–1995
Helen Stevenson Meyner	Dem.-N.J.	1975–1979
Virginia Dodd Smith	Rep.-Nebr.	1975–1991
Gladys Noon Spellman	Dem.-Md.	1975–1981
Shirley Neil Pettis	Rep.-Calif.	1975–1979
Barbara Ann Mikulski[1]	Dem.-Md.	1977–1987
May Rose Oakar	Dem.-Ohio	1977–1993
Beverly Barton Butcher Byron	Dem.-Md.	1979–1993
Geraldine Anne Ferraro	Dem.-N.Y.	1979–1985
Olympia Jean Snowe[1]	Rep.-Maine	1979–1995

1980–1989

Name	Party-State	Dates Served
Bobbi Fiedler	Rep.-Calif.	1981–1987
Lynn Morley Martin	Rep.-Ill.	1981–1991
Margaret Scafati Roukema	Rep.-N.J.	1981–2003
Claudine Schneider	Rep.-R.I.	1981–1991
Barbara Bailey Kennelly	Dem.-Conn.	1982–1999
Jean Spencer Ashbrook	Rep.-Ohio	1982–1983
Katie Beatrice Hall	Dem.-Ind.	1982–1985
Barbara Boxer[1]	Dem.-Calif.	1983–1993
Nancy Lee Johnson	Rep.-Conn.	1983–2007
Marcia Carolyn (Marcy) Kaptur	Dem.-Ohio	1983–
Barbara Farrell Vucanovich	Rep.-Nev.	1983–1997
Sala Burton	Dem.-Calif.	1983–1987
Helen Delich Bentley	Rep.-Md.	1985–1995
Jan Meyers	Rep.-Kans.	1985–1997
Catherine S. Long	Dem.-La.	1985–1987
Constance A. Morella	Rep.-Md.	1987–2003
Elizabeth J. Patterson	Dem.-S.C.	1987–1993
Patricia Fukuda Saiki	Rep.-Hawaii	1987–1991
Louise M. Slaughter	Dem.-N.Y.	1987–
Nancy Pelosi	Dem.-Calif.	1987–

Nita M. Lowey	Dem.-N.Y.	1989–
Jolene Unsoeld	Dem.-Wash.	1989–1995
Jill Long	Dem.-Ind.	1989–1995
Ileana Ros-Lehtinen	Rep.-Fla.	1989–

1990–1999

Name	Party-State	Dates Served
Susan Molinari	Rep.-N.Y.	1990–1997
Barbara-Rose Collins	Dem.-Mich.	1991–1997
Rosa L. DeLauro	Dem.-Conn.	1991–
Joan Kelly Horn	Dem.-Mo.	1991–1993
Eleanor Holmes Norton[2]	Dem.-D.C.	1991–
Maxine Waters	Dem.-Calif.	1991–
Eva Clayton	Dem.-N.C.	1992–2003
Corinne Brown	Dem.-Fla.	1993–
Leslie Byrne	Dem.-Va.	1993–1995
Maria Cantwell	Dem.-Wash.	1993–1995
Pat Danner	Dem.-Mo.	1993–2001
Jennifer Dunn	Rep.-Wash.	1993–2005
Karan English	Dem-Ariz.	1993–1995
Anna G. Eshoo	Dem.-Calif.	1993–
Tillie Fowler	Rep.-Fla.	1993–2001
Elizabeth Furse	Dem.-Ore.	1993–1999
Jane Harman	Dem.-Calif.	1993–1999; 2001–
Eddie Bernice Johnson	Dem.-Tex.	1993–
Blanche Lambert Lincoln[1]	Dem.-Ark.	1993–1997
Carolyn B. Maloney	Dem.-N.Y.	1993–
Marjorie Margolies-Mezvinsky	Dem.-Pa.	1993–1995
Cynthia McKinney	Dem.-Ga.	1993–2003; 2005–2007
Carrie P. Meek	Dem.-Fla.	1993–2003
Deborah Pryce	Rep.-Ohio	1993–
Lucille Roybal-Allard	Dem.-Calif.	1993–
Lynn Schenk	Dem.-Calif.	1993–1995
Karen Shepherd	Dem.-Utah	1993–1995
Karen Thurman	Dem.-Fla.	1993–2003
Nydia M. Velázquez	Dem.-N.Y.	1993–
Lynn Woolsey	Dem.-Calif.	1993–

Helen Chenoweth-Hage	Rep.-Idaho	1995–2001
Barbara Cubin	Rep.-Wyo.	1995–
Sheila Jackson-Lee	Dem.-Tex.	1995–
Sue Kelly	Rep.-N.Y.	1995–2007
Zoe Lofgren	Dem.-Calif.	1995–
Karen McCarthy	Dem.-Mo.	1995–2005
Sue Myrick	Rep.-N.C.	1995–
Lynn Rivers	Dem.-Mich.	1995–2003
Andrea Seastrand	Rep.-Calif.	1995–1997
Linda Smith	Rep.-Wash.	1995–1999
Enid Greene (Waldholtz)	Rep.-Utah	1995–1997
Juanita Millender-McDonald	Dem.-Calif.	1996–
Jo Ann Emerson	Rep.-Mo.	1996–
Julia Carson	Dem.-Ind.	1997–
Donna M. C. Christensen[2]	Dem.-Virgin Isl.	1997–
Diana DeGette	Dem.-Colo.	1997–
Kay Granger	Rep.-Tex.	1997–
Darlene Hooley	Dem.-Ore.	1997–
Carolyn Cheeks Kilpatrick	Dem.-Mich.	1997–
Carolyn McCarthy	Dem.-N.Y.	1997–
Anne Northup	Rep.-Ky.	1997–
Loretta Sanchez	Dem.-Calif.	1997–
Debbie Stabenow[1]	Dem.-Mich.	1997–2001
Ellen Tauscher	Dem.-Calif.	1997–
Mary Bono	Rep.-Calif.	1998–
Lois Capps	Dem.-Calif.	1998–
Barbara Lee	Dem.-Calif.	1998–
Heather Wilson	Rep.-N.M.	1998–
Tammy Baldwin	Dem.-Wis.	1999–
Shelley Berkley	Dem.-Nev.	1999–
Judith Borg Biggert	Rep.-Ill.	1999–
Stephanie Tubbs Jones	Dem.-Ohio	1999–
Grace Napolitano	Dem-Calif.	1999–
Janice Schakowsky	Dem.-Ill.	1999–

2000–2007

Name	Party-State	Dates Served
Shelley Moore Capito	Rep.-W. Va.	2001–
Jo Ann Davis	Rep.-Va.	2001–

Susan A. Davis	Dem.-Calif.	2001–
Melissa Hart	Rep.-Pa.	2001–2007
Betty McCollum	Dem.-Minn.	2001–
Hilda Solis	Dem.-Calif.	2001–
Diane Watson	Dem.-Calif.	2001–
Marsha Blackburn	Rep.-Tenn.	2003–
Madeleine Bordallo	Dem.-Guam	2003–
Ginny Brown-Waite	Rep.-Fla.	2003–
Katherine Harris	Rep.-Fla.	2003–2007
Denise Majette	Dem.-Ga.	2003–2005
Candice Miller	Rep.-Mich.	2003–
Marilyn Musgrave	Rep.-Colo.	2003–
Linda Sanchez	Dem.-Calif.	2003–
Stephanie Herseth	Dem.-S.D.	2004–
Melissa Bean	Dem.-Ill.	2005–
Thelma Drake	Rep.-Va.	2005–
Virginia Foxx	Rep.-N.C.	2005–
Cathy McMorris	Rep.-Wash.	2005–
Gwen Moore	Dem.-Wis.	2005–
Allyson Schwartz	Dem.-Pa.	2005–
Debbie Wasserman-Schultz	Dem.-Fla.	2005–
Doris Matsui	Dem.-Calif.	2005–
Jean Schmidt	Rep.-Ohio	2005–
Shelly Sekula-Gibbs	Rep.-Tex.	2006–2007
Michele Bachmann	Rep.-Minn.	2007–
Nancy Boyda	Dem.-Kans.	2007–
Kathy Castor	Dem.-Fla.	2007–
Yvette Clarke	Dem.-N.Y.	2007–
Mary Fallin	Dem.-Okla.	2007–
Gabrielle Giffords	Dem.-Ariz.	2007–
Kirsten Gillibrand	Dem.-N.Y.	2007–
Mazie K. Hirono	Dem.-Hawaii	2007–
Carol Shea-Porter	Dem.-N.H.	2007–
Betty Sutton	Dem.-Ohio	2007–

1. Went on to serve in the U.S. Senate.
2. Nonvoting delegate to Congress.
Source: Fact Monster/Information Please® Database, © 2007 Pearson Education, Inc.

Appendix II

SPEAKERS OF THE HOUSE

Article I, Section 2, of the Constitution states: *"The House of Representatives shall chuse their Speaker and other Officers."* And when Congress first convened in 1789, the House chose Frederick A. C. Muhlenberg as its Speaker. The Speaker acts as leader of the House and combines several roles: the institutional role of presiding officer and administrative head of the House, the partisan role of leader of the majority party in the House, and the representative role of an elected Member of the House. The Speaker of the House is second in line to succeed the president. Information on the current Speaker is available at the Web site of the Speaker of the House, www.speaker.gov

Speakers of the House

Congress	Speaker	State	Date Elected
1st	Frederick A.C. Muhlenberg	Pennsylvania	Apr. 1, 1789
2nd	Jonathan Trumbull	Connecticut	Oct. 24, 1791
3rd	Frederick A.C. Muhlenberg	Pennsylvania	Dec. 2, 1793
4th	Jonathan Dayton	New Jersey	Dec. 7, 1795
5th	Jonathan Dayton	New Jersey	May 15, 1797
6th	Theodore Sedgwick	Massachusetts	Dec. 2, 1799
7th	Nathaniel Macon	North Carolina	Dec. 7, 1801
8th	Nathaniel Macon	North Carolina	Oct. 17, 1803
9th	Nathaniel Macon	North Carolina	Dec. 2, 1805

Congress	Speaker	State	Date Elected
10th	Joseph B. Varnum	Massachusetts	Oct. 26, 1807
11th	Joseph B. Varnum	Massachusetts	May 22, 1809
12th	Henry Clay	Kentucky	Nov. 4, 1811
13th	Henry Clay[1]	Kentucky	May 24, 1813
13th	Langdon Cheves	South Carolina	Jan. 19, 1814
14th	Henry Clay	Kentucky	Dec. 4, 1815
15th	Henry Clay	Kentucky	Dec. 1, 1817
16th	Henry Clay[2]	Kentucky	Dec. 6, 1819
16th	John W. Taylor	New York	Nov. 15, 1820
17th	Philip P. Barbour	Virginia	Dec. 4, 1821
18th	Henry Clay[3]	Kentucky	Dec. 1, 1823
19th	John W. Taylor	New York	Dec. 5, 1825
20th	Andrew Stevenson	Virginia	Dec. 3, 1827
21st	Andrew Stevenson	Virginia	Dec. 7, 1829
22nd	Andrew Stevenson	Virginia	Dec. 5, 1831
23rd	John Bell	Tennessee	June 2, 1834
24th	James K. Polk	Tennessee	Dec. 7, 1835
25th	James K. Polk	Tennessee	Sept. 4, 1837
26th	Robert M.T. Hunter	Virginia	Dec. 16, 1839
27th	John White	Kentucky	May 31, 1841
28th	John W. Jones	Virginia	Dec. 4, 1843
29th	John W. Davis	Indiana	Dec. 1, 1845
30th	Robert C. Winthrop	Massachusetts	Dec. 6, 1847
31st	Howell Cobb	Georgia	Dec. 22, 1849
32nd	Linn Boyd	Kentucky	Dec. 1, 1851
33rd	Linn Boyd	Kentucky	Dec. 5, 1853
34th	Nathaniel P. Banks	Massachusetts	Feb. 2, 1856
35th	James L. Orr	South Carolina	Dec. 7, 1857
36th	William Pennington	New Jersey	Feb. 1, 1860
37th	Galusha A. Grow	Pennsylvania	July 4, 1861
38th	Schuyler Colfax	Indiana	Dec. 7, 1863
39th	Schuyler Colfax	Indiana	Dec. 4, 1865
40th	Schuyler Colfax	Indiana	Mar. 4, 1867
40th	Theodore M. Pomeroy[4]	New York	Mar. 3, 1869

Congress	Speaker	State	Date Elected
41st	James G. Blaine	Maine	Mar. 4, 1869
42nd	James G. Blaine	Maine	Mar. 4, 1871
43rd	James G. Blaine	Maine	Dec. 1, 1873
44th	Michael C. Kerr[5]	Indiana	Dec. 6, 1875
44th	Samuel J. Randall	Pennsylvania	Dec. 4, 1876
45th	Samuel J. Randall	Pennsylvania	Dec. 4, 1876
46th	Samuel J. Randal	Pennsylvania	Mar. 18, 1879
47th	J. Warren Keifer	Ohio	Dec. 5, 1881
48th	John G. Carlisle	Kentucky	Dec. 3, 1883
49th	John G. Carlisle	Kentucky	Dec. 7, 1885
50th	John G. Carlisle	Kentucky	Dec. 5, 1887
51st	Thomas B. Reed	Maine	Dec. 2, 1889
52nd	Charles F. Crisp	Georgia	Dec. 8, 1891
53rd	Charles F. Crisp	Georgia	Aug. 7, 1893
54th	Thomas B. Reed	Maine	Dec. 2, 1895
55th	Thomas B. Reed	Maine	Mar. 15, 1897
56th	David B. Henderson	Iowa	Dec. 4, 1899
57th	David B. Henderson	Iowa	Dec. 2, 1901
58th	Joseph G. Cannon	Illinois	Nov. 9, 1903
59th	Joseph G. Cannon	Illinois	Dec. 4, 1905
60th	Joseph G. Cannon	Illinois	Dec. 2, 1907
61st	Joseph G. Cannon	Illinois	Mar. 15, 1909
62nd	James Beauchamp Clark	Missouri	Apr. 4, 1911
63rd	James Beauchamp Clark	Missouri	Apr. 7, 1913
64th	James Beauchamp Clark	Missouri	Dec. 6, 1915
65th	James Beauchamp Clark	Missouri	Apr. 2, 1917
66th	Frederick H. Gillett	Massachusetts	May 19, 1919
67th	Frederick H. Gillett	Massachusetts	Apr. 11, 1921
68th	Frederick H. Gillett	Massachusetts	Dec. 3, 1923
69th	Nicholas Longworth	Ohio	Dec. 7, 1925
70th	Nicholas Longworth	Ohio	Dec. 5, 1927
71st	Nicholas Longworth	Ohio	Apr. 15, 1929
72nd	John N. Garner	Texas	Dec. 7, 1931
73rd	Henry T. Rainey[6]	Illinois	Mar. 9, 1933

Congress	Speaker	State	Date Elected
74th	Joseph W. Byrns[7]	Tennessee	Jan. 3, 1935
74th	William B. Bankhead	Alabama	Jun. 4, 1936
75th	William B. Bankhead	Alabama	Jan. 5, 1937
76th	William B. Bankhead[8]	Alabama	Jan. 3, 1939
76th	Sam Rayburn	Texas	Sept. 16, 1940
77th	Sam Rayburn	Texas	Jan. 3, 1941
78th	Sam Rayburn	Texas	Jan. 6, 1943
79th	Sam Rayburn	Texas	Jan. 3, 1945
80th	Joseph W. Martin, Jr.	Massachusetts	Jan. 3, 1947
81st	Sam Rayburn	Texas	Jan. 3, 1949
82nd	Sam Rayburn	Texas	Jan. 3, 1951
83rd	Joseph W. Martin, Jr.	Massachusetts	Jan. 3, 1953
84th	Sam Rayburn	Texas	Jan. 5, 1955
85th	Sam Rayburn	Texas	Jan. 3, 1957
86th	Sam Rayburn	Texas	Jan. 7, 1959
87th	Sam Rayburn[9]	Texas	Jan. 3, 1961
87th	John W. McCormack	Massachusetts	Jan. 10, 1962
88th	John W. McCormack	Massachusetts	Jan. 9, 1963
89th	John W. McCormack	Massachusetts	Jan. 4, 1965
90th	John W. McCormack	Massachusetts	Jan. 10, 1967
91st	John W. McCormack	Massachusetts	Jan. 3, 1969
92nd	Carl B. Albert	Oklahoma	Jan. 21, 1971
93rd	Carl B. Albert	Oklahoma	Jan. 3, 1973
94th	Carl B. Albert	Oklahoma	Jan. 14, 1975
95th	Thomas P. O'Neill, Jr.	Massachusetts	Jan. 4, 1977
96th	Thomas P. O'Neill, Jr.	Massachusetts	Jan. 15, 1979
97th	Thomas P. O'Neill, Jr.	Massachusetts	Jan. 5, 1981
98th	Thomas P. O'Neill, Jr.	Massachusetts	Jan. 3, 1983
99th	Thomas P. O'Neill, Jr.	Massachusetts	Jan. 3, 1985
100th	James C. Wright, Jr.	Texas	Jan. 6, 1987
101st	James C. Wright, Jr.[10]	Texas	Jan. 3, 1989
101st	Thomas S. Foley	Washington	Jun. 6, 1989
102nd	Thomas S. Foley	Washington	Jan. 3, 1991
103rd	Thomas S. Foley	Washington	Jan. 5, 1993

Congress	Speaker	State	Date Elected
104th	Newt Gingrich	Georgia	Jan. 4, 1995
105th	Newt Gingrich	Georgia	Jan. 7, 1997
106th	J. Dennis Hastert	Illinois	Jan. 6, 1999
107th	J. Dennis Hastert	Illinois	Jan. 3, 2001
108th	J. Dennis Hastert	Illinois	Jan. 7, 2003
109th	J. Dennis Hastert	Illinois	Jan. 4, 2005
110th	Nancy Pelosi	California	Jan. 4, 2007

[1] Resigned from the House of Representatives, January 19, 1814.

[2] Resigned on October 28, 1820.

[3] Resigned from the House of Representatives, March 6, 1825.

[4] Elected Speaker, March 3, 1869, and served one day.

[5] Died in office, August 19, 1876.

[6] Died in office, August 19, 1934.

[7] Died in office June 4, 1936.

[8] Died in office, September 15, 1940.

[9] Died November 16, 1961.

[10] Resigned from the House of Representatives, June 6, 1989.

Source: Biographical Directory of the U.S. Congress, Congressional Research Service.

Appendix III

NANCY PELOSI'S FIRST SPEECH AS SPEAKER OF THE HOUSE OF REPRESENTATIVES (JANUARY 4, 2007)

"Thank you my colleagues, thank you leader [John] Boehner [R-Ohio].

"I accept this gavel in the spirit of partnership, not partisanship, and I look forward to working with you Mr. Boehner and the Republicans in the Congress on behalf of the American people.

"After giving away this gavel in the last two Congresses, I'm glad someone else had the honor today.

"In this House, we may belong to different parties, but we serve one country. We stand united in our pride and prayers for our men and women in the armed forces. They are working together to protect America, and we, in this House, must also work together to build a future worthy of their sacrifice.

"In this hour, we need and pray for the character, courage, and civility of a former member of this House—President Ford. He healed the country when it needed healing. This is another time, another war, and another trial of our American will, imagination, and spirit. Let us honor his memory, not just in eulogy, but in dialogue and trust across the aisle. Let us express our condolences and appreciation to Mrs. Ford and the entire Ford family for their decades of service to our country.

"With today's convening of the 110th Congress, we begin anew. I congratulate all members of Congress on your election; I especially want to congratulate our new members of Congress. The genius of our Founders was that every two years, new members bring to this House their spirit of renewal and hope for the American people. This Congress is reinvigorated new members by your optimism, your idealism, and your commitment to our country. Let us acknowledge your families, whose support has made your leadership possible.

"Each of us brings to this new Congress our shared values, our commitment to the Constitution, and our personal experience.

"My path to Congress and the speakership began in Baltimore where my father was mayor. I was raised in a large family that was devoutly Catholic, deeply patriotic, very proud of our Italian American heritage, and staunchly Democratic. My parents taught us that public service was a noble calling, and that we had a responsibility to help those in need. I viewed them as working on the side of the angels and now they are with them.

"I am so proud that my brother Tommy D'Alesandro, who was also a mayor of Baltimore, is here leading my D'Alesandro family today.

"Forty-three years ago, Paul Pelosi and I were married. We raised our five children in San Francisco, where Paul was born and raised. I want to thank Paul and our children Nancy Corinne, Christine, Jacqueline, Paul, and Alexandra and our six magnificent grandchildren for giving me their love, support and the confidence to go from the kitchen to the Congress.

"And I thank my constituents in San Francisco and to the state of California for the privilege of representing them in Congress. Saint Francis of Assisi is our city's patron saint, and his song of St. Francis is our city's anthem: 'Lord, make me a channel of thy peace; where there is darkness may we bring light, where there is hatred, may we bring love, and where there is despair, may we bring hope.'

"Hope, hope, that is what America is about and it is in that spirit that I was sent to Congress.

"And today, I thank my colleagues. By electing me speaker, you have brought us closer to the ideal of equality that is America's heritage and America's hope.

"This is an historic moment—and I thank the leader for acknowledging it. I think you Leader Boehner. It is an historic moment for the Congress, and an historic moment for the women of this country. It is a moment for which we have waited over 200 years. Never losing faith, we waited through the many years of struggle to achieve our rights. But women weren't just waiting; women were working. Never losing faith, we worked to redeem the promise of America, that all men and women are created equal. For our daughters and granddaughters, today we have broken the marble ceiling. For our daughters and our granddaughters, the sky is the limit, anything is possible for them.

"The election of 2006 was a call to change—not merely to change the control of Congress, but for a new direction for our country. Nowhere were the American people more clear about the need for a new direction than in the war in Iraq.

"The American people rejected an open-ended obligation to a war without end. Shortly, President Bush will address the nation on the subject of Iraq. It is the responsibility of the president to articulate a new plan for Iraq that makes it clear to the Iraqis that they must defend their own streets and their own security, a plan that promotes stability in the region, and a plan that allows us to responsibly redeploy our troops.

"Let us work together to be the Congress that rebuilds our military to meet the national security challenges of the 21st century.

"Let us be the Congress that strongly honors our responsibility to protect the American people from terrorism.

"Let us be the Congress that never forgets our commitment to our veterans and our first responders, always honoring them as the heroes that they are.

"The American people also spoke clearly for a new direction here at home—they desire a new vision, a new America, built on the values that have made our country great.

"Our founders envisioned a new America driven by optimism, opportunity, and strength. So confident were they in the America they were advancing, they put on the seal, the great seal of the United States, 'novus ordo seclorum'—a new order for the centuries. Centuries, they spoke of the centuries. They envisioned America as a just and good place, as a fair and efficient society, as a source of opportunity for all.

"This vision has sustained us for over 200 years, and it accounts for what is best in our great nation: liberty, opportunity, and justice.

"Now it is our responsibility to carry forth that vision of a new America into the 21st Century.

"A new America that seizes the future and forges 21st Century solutions through discovery, creativity, and innovation, sustaining our economic leadership and ensuring our national security.

"A new America with a vibrant and strengthened middle class for whom college is affordable, health care is accessible, and retirement reliable.

"A new America that declares our energy independence, promotes domestic sources of renewable energy, and combats climate change.

"A new America that is strong, secure, and a respected leader among the community of nations.

"And the American people told us they expected us to work together for fiscal responsibility, with the highest ethical standards and with civility and bipartisanship.

"After years of historic deficits, this 110th Congress will commit itself to a higher standard: pay as you go, no new deficit spending. Our new

America will provide unlimited opportunity for future generations, not burden them with mountains of debt.

"In order to achieve our new America for the 21st Century, we must return this House to the American people. So our first order of business is passing the toughest congressional ethics reform in history. This new Congress doesn't have two years or 200 days.

"Let us join together in the first 100 hours to make this Congress the most honest and open Congress in history—100 hours.

"This openness requires respect for every voice in the Congress. As Thomas Jefferson said, 'Every difference of opinion is not a difference of principle.' My colleagues elected me to be Speaker of the House—the entire House. Respectful of the vision of our Founders, the expectations of our people, and the great challenges that we face, we have an obligation to reach beyond partisanship to work for all Americans.

"Let us all stand together to move our country forward, seeking common ground for the common good.

"We have made history, now let us make progress for our the America people.

"May God bless our work, and may God bless America."

Source: Speech available at http://speaker.house.gov/newsroom/speeches?id=0006.

Appendix IV

AN INTERVIEW WITH NANCY PELOSI (JANUARY 2007)

Nancy Pelosi talks about her life, her children and grandchildren, and her priorities with Elaine S. Povich.

Q. Discuss your dual roles as mother/grandmother and speaker. How do you balance the two? How does being a grandmother influence your views on issues?

A. November was so exciting for me: Democrats had victories from coast to coast; my youngest daughter gave birth to my sixth grandchild; and my Democratic colleagues nominated me to represent them as Speaker.

I view my role in politics as an extension of my role as mother and grandmother. The reasons I came to Congress are simple: the children, the children, the children.

Being a grandmother is a constant reminder of the need to build a stronger future for the generations to come. That means protecting our precious environment, ensuring a good education and a wealth of opportunities for every American, and preventing our grandchildren from being burdened with mountains of debt.

Q. How did managing a household of five children affect your management style in Congress? Does the experience of managing your family help you make the diverse personalities and interests of House members into a cohesive family?

A. Having five children in six years is the best training in the world for speaker of the house. When my children were young, time was my most precious commodity. It made me the ultimate multitasker and the master of focus, routine and scheduling.

The House Democratic Caucus is blessed by the diversity of its members. Just as I do as a mother, as Speaker, I intend to do a great deal of listening. But, when necessary, I am not afraid to use my mother-of-five voice to ensure that I am heard.

Q. How confident are you that the Congress and the president can agree on a plan to strengthen Social Security? What ideas do you favor: Raising the ceiling on taxed income? Raising the eligibility age? Private accounts funded by payroll taxes? Trimming benefits?

A. The Republican privatization plan has already been rejected by the American people and will go nowhere in a Democratic Congress. It is bad policy that would drain trillions of dollars from the Social Security trust fund, increase the national debt, and slash future retiree benefits by more than 40 percent.

Social Security does face problems down the road, and we need to solve them, but we have the time to do it right. Democrats want to work with Republicans in a bipartisan way to make adjustments to keep Social Security solvent after the year 2050.

Q. What steps will the House take to reduce the number of uninsured Americans and to cut the cost of health care?

A. Making health care more accessible and affordable is one of the greatest challenges facing our nation, but Democrats believe that the wealthiest nation in the world should also be the healthiest. We are prepared to get right to work.

There are real opportunities for solutions to reach our goal of making health care more affordable. Health technology can mean better care, lower costs, less hassle, and fewer mistakes. Reorienting our priorities to promote prevention can lower the vast amount of health expenditures incurred by chronic care. And by investing in research we can demonstrate which drug, device, or medical procedure works best.

Q. Will the House support the president's call for an entitlements commission [to devise ways to shore up Social Security and Medicare]?

A. The health of our nation has been endangered by the fiscal irresponsibility of President Bush and congressional Republicans, who have burdened our future generations with mountains of debt.

House Democrats will take our nation in a new direction of fiscal responsibility, following the strict rules of no new deficit budgeting. As such, we will have to make difficult decisions by examining the entire budget. All federal departments and agencies should be able to take an audit.

I would be reluctant to support calls for an entitlements commission, especially if it did not include a hard look at the policies that caused our mounting debt.

Q. Before the November [2006] elections, voters age 50-plus rated corruption as the single most important issue. How much control do you think the Speaker has over the behavior of members of Congress? How will the House meet the public concerns for stronger ethics protection?

A. The first order of business for the Democratic Congress will be ethics reform to ensure legislative decisions are made for the common good. Democrats will break the link between lobbyists and legislation, which will mean that we can govern for all Americans, not just the privileged few. Reform will be instrumental to passing legislation that makes prescription drugs more affordable and ends giveaways to Big Oil.

Q. How can Congress reduce energy prices and our dependence on oil?

Democrats are taking the first step toward energy independence by rolling back billions of dollars of subsidies for Big Oil already making record profits, and investing in renewable energy and energy efficiency to help wean us off of foreign oil.

Source: This interview first appeared in *AARP Bulletin* in January 2007.

SELECTED BIBLIOGRAPHY

BOOKS

Barone, Michael. *The Almanac of American Politics 2004*. National Journal Inc., 2003.

Barone, Michael, and Grant Ujifusa. *The Almanac of American Politics 1988*. National Journal Inc., 1987.

———. *The Almanac of American Politics 1900*. National Journal Inc., 1989.

———. *The Almanac of American Politics 1992*. National Journal Inc., 1991.

———. *The Almanac of American Politics 1994*. National Journal Inc., 1993.

———. *The Almanac of American Politics 1996*. National Journal Inc., 1995.

———. *The Almanac of American Politics 1998*. National Journal Inc., 1997.

Barone, Michael, with Richard E. Cohen. *The Almanac of American Politics 2002*. National Journal Inc., 2001.

Barone, Michael, and Richard E. Cohen. *The Almanac of American Politics 2006*. National Journal Inc., 2005.

Boxer, Barbara, with Nicole Boxer. *Strangers in the Senate; Politics and the New Revolution of Women in America*. National Press Books, 1994.

Duncan, Phil, and the CQ Political Staff. *Congressional Quarterly's Politics in America 1988, the 100th Congress*. CQ Press, 1987.

———. *Congressional Quarterly's Politics in America 1990, the 101st Congress*. CQ Press, 1989.

———. *Congressional Quarterly's Politics in America 1992, the 102nd Congress*. CQ Press, 1991.

———. *Politics in America 1994, the 103rd Congress*. CQ Press, 1993.

Duncan, Phil, and the Staff of Congressional Quarterly. *CQ's Politics in America, 1996, the 104th Congress*. CQ Press, 1995.

Duncan, Phil, and Christine C. Lawrence. *CQ's Politics in America, 1998, the 105th Congress.* CQ Press, 1997.

Duncan, Philip, and Brian Nutting, eds. *CQ's Politics in America 2000, the 106th Congress.* CQ Press, 1999.

Hawkings, David, and Brian Nutting, eds., and Congressional Quarterly Staff. *CQ's Politics in America 2004, the 108th Congress.* CQ Press, 2003.

Jacobs, John. *A Rage for Justice: The Passion and Politics of Phillip Burton.* University of California Press, 1997.

Koszczuk, Jackie, and H. Amy Stern, eds., and the Congressional Quarterly Staff. *CQ's Politics in America 2006, the 109th Congress.* CQ Press, 2005.

Lawrence, Christine, ed. *Congressional Quarterly's Politics in America 1998, the 105th Congress.* CQ Press, 1997.

Nutting, Brian, and H. Amy Stern, eds. *CQ's Politics in America 2002, the 107th Congress.* CQ Press, 2001.

Sandler, Gilbert. *The Neighborhood, The Story of Baltimore's Little Italy.* Bodine & Associates, 1974.

PERIODICALS

Cocco, Marie. "This Is What a Speaker Looks Like." *Ms. Magazine* (Winter 2007).

The Congressional Record, Oct. 18, 1989.

The Congressional Record, Oct. 23, 1989.

The Congressional Record, Dec. 18, 2007.

Eilperin, Juliet. "The Making of Madam Whip: Fear and Loathing—and Horse Trading—in the Race for the House's No. 2 Democrat." *Washington Post Magazine,* January 6, 2002, p. W27.

Ferrell, Jane. "A Highly Conventional Democrat." *California Living Magazine,* January 15, 1984, pp. 8–12.

Feurerherd, Joe. Interview of Nancy Pelosi. *The National Catholic Reporter,* January 24, 2003.

Lewis, Peggy. "Profile: Nancy Pelosi '62: House Democratic Leader." *Trinity College Magazine,* 2002.

Lewis, Peggy. "Profile: Nancy Pelosi '62 House Democratic Leader." *Trinity Magazine,* Fall 2003.

"The Little World of Tommy." *Time Magazine,* April 26, 1954.

Meyerson, Harold. "How Nancy Pelosi Took Control: The San Francisco Liberal Turns Out to Be a Tough Customer." *The American Prospect,* May 12, 2004.

Skidmore, David, and William Gates. "After Tiananmen: The Struggle over U.S. Policy toward China in the Bush Administration." *Presidential Studies Quarterly* 27 (1997).

Tumulty, Karen, and Perry Bacon Jr. "Did Nancy Pelosi Get the Message?" *Time Magazine,* November 19, 2006.

NEWSPAPERS

Atlanta Journal Constitution
Baltimore Sun
Chicago Sun-Times
Chicago Tribune
Los Angeles Times
New York Daily News
New York Times
Newsday
San Francisco Chronicle
San Francisco Examiner
San Jose Mercury News
Wall Street Journal
Washington Post

WEB SITES (OTHER THAN NEWSPAPERS)

Office of Rep. Nancy Pelosi: http://www.house.gov/pelosi.

Office of the Speaker of the House: http://speaker.gov/.

The Library of Congress: http://www.loc.gov.

National Park Service: www.nps.gov, "The Presidio of San Francisco," U.S. Military Period, 1846–1994.

"Search the Quilt," feature: www.aidsquilt.org.

Almanac of American Politics online version, June 22, 2005, update: http://nationaljournal.com/pubs/almanac/2006/people/mi/rep_mi15.htm.

House Ethics Committee, Historical Chart: www.house.gov/ethics/Historical_chart_Final_Version.htm.

Terrorfile online, The assassination of Bishop Juan Jose Gerardi: http://www.terrorfile online.org/en/index.php/The_Assassination_of_Bishop_Juan_Jose_Gerardi.

Rutgers, the State University of New Jersey, Thomas Eagleton Institute of Politics: http://www.eagleton.rutgers.edu/e-gov/e-politicalarchive-2000.htm.

Democratic Daily, January 3, 2007: http://thedemocraticdaily.com.

BROADCAST SOURCES

ABC News, "Streisand Hosts Pelosi at Fundraiser," April 13, 2007. Available at http://abcnews.go.com/Entertainment/wireStory?id=3039412/.

CNN, March 9, 2001, http://archives.cnn.com/2001/ALLPOLITICS/03/09/bush. budget/index.html.

CNN.com, October 11, 2002, http://archives.cnn.com/2002/ALLPOLITICS/10/11/iraq.us/.

David Paul Kuhn, "'Mission Accomplished' Revisited." CBS News.com, April 30, 2004.

Diane Sawyer and Robin Roberts, "Madam Speaker, What Does Pelosi Mean for Women?" *Good Morning America*, ABC News, January 5, 2007.

Katie Couric, interview with Nancy Pelosi, *Today* Show, NBC, January 4, 2005.

Lesley Stahl, interview of Nancy Pelosi, *60 Minutes*, CBS, October 22, 2006.

MacNeil/Lehrer News Hour, PBS.

Ron Elving, "Congress, 10 years after the Gingrich Revolution." National Public Radio, Jan. 11, 2005.

Tavis Smiley, PBS.

INDIVIDUAL INTERVIEWS

Thomas D'Alesandro III

Martha Buonanno

John Burton

Mario Cuomo

Frank DeFilippo

Former Rep. Martin Frost

Former Rep. Sam Gejdensen

Angie Guerriero

John Guerriero

Rep. Steny Hoyer, D-Md.

Agar Jaicks

Sally Laughland

Naomi Lauter

Sam Lauter

Rep. George Miller, D-Calif.

Former Sen. George Mitchell, D-Maine (e-mail)

Ed Moose

Steve Morin

Cressey H. Nakagawa

Christine Pelosi

Rep. Nancy Pelosi, D.-Calif. (e-mail)

John Pente

Gilbert Sandler

Michael Yaki

INDEX

Sanchez, Loretta, 114
Sandler, Gilbert, 3, 4
Schroeder, Patricia, 98
Schumer, Charles, 111
Select Committee on
    Intelligence, 73–74, 77–80
September, 11, 2001 attacks, 65,
    74, 78–79, 88, 91–92
Sisters of Notre Dame de
    Namur, 9
Smoking ban, 118
Spellman, Gladys Noon, 84
Stahl, Lesley, 80
Sullivan, John, 45

Tauscher, Ellen, 85
Tiananmen Square protest, 53–57
Title IX, 98

Trinity College (University), 6,
    9–13, 101, 112, 113
Tsongas, Niki, 71, 121

Velazquez, Nydia, 119
Vos, Michiel, 111
Vos, Paul Michael, 111
Vos, Thomas Vincent, 120

Whip, 81–89, 95, 98, 112
Wilson, Charlie, 77
Wright, Jim, 37, 74–75, 82

Yaki, Michael, 32, 45–46, 55–56
Yard, Molly, 99

Zemin, Jiang, 58
Zuur, Ted, 34

About the Author

ELAINE S. POVICH is an award-winning freelance journalist and veteran Washington correspondent who has reported for *UPI*, *Newsday*, the *Chicago Tribune*, and other news organizations, and written feature articles for many magazines and journals. She is the recipient of the Everett McKinley Dirksen Award for Distinguished Reporting of Congress. She is also the author of *Partners and Adversaries: The Contentious Connection between Congress and the Media* (1996), she is a member of the Gridiron Club, Washington's oldest journalistic organization, and is a past president of the Washington Press Club Foundation.